The Tradition of Workers' Control

FREEDOM PRESS publish *Freedom* (fortnightly) and *The Raven* (quarterly) as well as books (more than sixty titles in print).

FREEDOM PRESS BOOKSHOP carries the most comprehensive stock of anarchist literature, including titles from North America. Please send for our current list.

**Freedom Press
in Angel Alley
84b Whitechapel High Street
London
E1 7QX**

The Tradition of Workers' Control

selected writings by
Geoffrey Ostergaard

edited with an introduction by
Brian Bamford

FREEDOM PRESS
London

Published by
FREEDOM PRESS
84b Whitechapel High Street
London E1 7QX
1997

© Freedom Press 1997

ISBN 0 900384 91 3

Typeset by Jayne Clementson
Printed in Great Britain by Aldgate Press, London E1

Contents

Geoffrey Ostergaard: the official life	7
About Brian Bamford	9
British Syndicalism Through the Ages	11
The Tradition of Workers' Control	27
British Syndicalism	37
Syndicalist Controversies	47
Disintegration of the Syndicalist Movement	52
Guild Socialism	55
Guild Socialism Re-Stated	67
The Building Guilds	73
The Contribution of Guild Socialism	77
From Control to Consultation	80
The Tradition Survives	86
Fabianism and the Managerial Revolution	95
Industry and the Managerial Society	105
Socialism by Pressure Group	117
Fabian and Parliamentary Socialism	123
Modernity and its Aftermath	133
Appendix I: What's To Be Done	141
Appendix II: Anarchism and Syndicalism	146

Geoffrey Ostergaard: The Official Life

Geoffrey Nielsen Ostergaard was born on 25th July 1926 near Huntingdon. His father was a Danish immigrant and his mother died when he was five. He had a hard childhood, but won scholarships to Huntingdon Grammar School and then to Peterhouse, Cambridge. His education was interrupted by the war, and after training as a pilot he spent two years in the Royal Air Force. After the war he went to Merton College, Oxford, where he got a first-class degree in Philosophy, Politics and Economics in 1950. In 1948 he married Eva Dryden, and they had a son, Magnus.

Geoffrey spent the whole of his career as a full-time academic. He began as a research student at Nuffield College, Oxford, working under the great socialist scholar G.D.H. Cole, and he got his doctorate with a thesis on 'Public Ownership in Great Britain: A Study in the Development of Socialist Ideas' (1953). He then spent 37 years in the Department of Political Science at Birmingham University – becoming an assistant lecturer in 1953, a lecturer in 1955, and a senior lecturer in 1965. He was acting head of the department in 1965-66, and at various times he was a Rockefeller Foundation fellow at the University of California, Berkeley, and a visiting professor at Osmania University, Hyderabad, and an examiner for various faculties and boards.

Geoffrey contributed frequently to academic periodicals and symposia and occasionally to ordinary periodicals. He produced several essays and papers, and also some more substantial publications – *Co-operative Democracy* (1955) with J.A. Banks, *Constitutional Relations Between the Co-operative and Labour Parties* (1960) with B. Smith, *Latter-day Anarchism* (1964), *Power in Co-operatives* (1965) with A.H. Halsey, *Gandhian Nonviolence* (1978), and *Resisting the Nation State* (1982). Above all he produced two authoritative books – *The Gentle Anarchists* (1971) with Melville Currell, and *Nonviolent Revolution in India* (1985) – on the libertarian aspects of the Gandhian movement in India, which he had studied at length and at first hand.

Geoffrey was also a frequent contributor to the anarchist and pacifist press, sometimes writing over the anagram Gaston Gerard, and he was a valued trustee of the Commonweal Collection, *Peace News*, and the Friends of Freedom Press. He was a consistent defender of academic freedom, and also a guide, philosopher and friend to generations of anarchists and pacifists. Everyone who knew him liked him, and all his many friends will miss him. He died in Birmingham on 22nd March 1990. Obituaries appeared in *The Times*, *The Independent* (by A.H. Halsey) and *The Guardian* (by Colin Ward).

NW

Acknowledgements

Since I became involved in the anarchist movement in 1960, after the strike of engineering apprentices in May of that year, I have discussed the issues outlined here with many anarchist activists and trade union militants both in Britain and Spain. In particular I should like to thank James Pinkerton, secretary of the Syndicalist Workers' Federation until 1963; Peter Turner, *Freedom* editor and secretary of the SWF in the early 1970s; James Petty, secretary of the Direct Action Movement in the 1980s, for their help and advice over the years. I, of course, am responsible for the thrust of the analysis, and for any mistakes therein.

BB

About Brian Bamford

Brian Bamford became an anarchist in 1960, following his experiences in the national strike of engineering apprentices in May of that year. He joined the Syndicalist Workers' Federation, and helped organise another strike of engineering apprentices in November 1964.

Internationally, he went to Spain in the early 1960s, working as an electrician in a fishing village while operating as an informant and contact for the FIJL – Spanish Libertarian Youth. Later, in 1964, he affiliated to the Gibraltar Labour Union (anarcho-syndicalist), but the British government black-listed him, preventing him from working for either HM Government or those private companies with contracts with the British government. He was dismissed as an electrician at the airport.

In 1970, together with Bob Lees the Oldham anarcho-syndicalist, and the Manchester Anarchist Syndicalist Alliance, he launched the Campaign for Shop Stewards in Textiles. The catalyst for this was a strike of Asian workers at Arrow Mill (Courtaulds) in Rochdale where Bamford worked. This caused disruption in the local industry and inside the National Union of Textile & Allied Workers. The right to shopfloor representation was won, but both Bamford and Lees were sacked and expelled from the union.

During the Gibraltar General Strike of 1986, and the shipyard riots of 1987 in Puerto Real, Bamford was back in Andalucia working as an electrician and shop steward for Gibraltar Shiprepair. He has had a long association with José Netto, the Gibraltarian anarcho-syndicalist and former leader of the T&GWU in Gibraltar, and is a friend of Pépé Gomez, the anarchist militant in Puerto Real.

Bamford has been an industrial correspondent for *Freedom* since the 1960s, but more recently has been identified with the Campaign Against the Job Seeker's Act.

British Syndicalism through the ages: Geoffrey Ostergaard reconsidered

Anarchists have no need to steal Geoffrey Ostergaard: he was a committed anarchist throughout most of his life. He was not the sort of semi-detached intellectual who occasionally toys with anarchism when affecting a certain rhetorical poise such as A.J.P. Taylor, the historian, and James Cameron, the journalist.

Geoffrey Ostergaard was a historian of labour history who used an anarcho-syndicalist perspective. He was much else besides. He was Senior Lecturer in Government at the University of Birmingham. He had researched widely on the co-operative movement. In later years he contributed two major books on the Gandhian movement in India (he was a visiting professor at Osmania University, Hyderabad) using an anarchist framework to elucidate the cultural and religious roots of the Indian experience.

Academics and the Party Line

In an appreciation, written shortly after Mr Ostergaard's death in 1990, Colin Ward described him in the following terms: "In many respects he was the ideal anarchist academic, as he explored issues which we as propagandists found difficult, just because what actually happened didn't entirely conform to our theories." (*Freedom*, 7th April 1990)

As the anarchist movement is blessed by not having an official party line I suppose the Geoffrey Ostergaard ideal anarchist intellectual, as outlined by Colin Ward above, is the objective every aspiring anarchist pundit should aim at. Mr Ward also refers to Geoffrey's "moral staunchness" as remembered by former colleagues and students, and his steadfast support for academic freedom and unpopular causes such as that of David Selbourne at Ruskin College in the late 1980s.

The anarchist intellectual has to act in an arena of ideas and morals without ideological props and without much in the way of a script as a guide, save the maxim of anti-authoritarianism.

In contrast with marxism, anarchism doesn't have an institutional character. There is no head office for anarchism which can lay down ideas to be followed or a party line for anarchists. A true marxist can and often does profess beliefs he does not understand. As the marxist Leszek Kolakowski pointed out in his book *Marxism and Beyond* (1969): "The 1950 marxist knew that Lysenko's theory of heredity was correct, that Hegel represented the aristocratic reaction to the French Revolution, that Dostoevski was a decadent and Babaevski a great writer. That Suvorov served the cause of progress, and also the resonance theory in chemistry was reactionary nonsense. Every 1950 marxist knew these things even if he had never heard of chromosomes, had no idea what century Hegel lived in, had never read one of Dostoevski's books or studied a high-school chemistry textbook." Such toil would be unnecessary so long as the content of marxism is decided by what Leszek Kolakowski calls "the office".

Of course Mr Kolakowski, though he was expelled from the Polish Communist Party in 1966, was still a marxist in 1969 and keen to rescue marxism by saying that besides "institutional marxism" there is a genuine intellectual marxist current. And that this intellectual marxism would become a 'permanent aspect' absorbed into the social sciences, while 'institutional marxism' – head office marxism – would become an increasingly transitory aspect.

Unfortunately these two aspects of marxism have not been so easily separated. A distinguished historian like Eric J. Hobsbawm, respected by the liberal academic establishment, now appears to us like one of those Catholic priests who never believed in God all the time, is claiming that the Soviet Union (the marxist 'Vatican', head office until 1989) was never held in such high esteem by western marxists. Today he says they were only pretending to believe in 'office marxism' and he even has the brass-neck to argue that the October 'Russian Revolution' was more 'anarchist' in its inspired insurrectionary style than marxist.

Clearly anarchism can't compete with the simplified mind-set of the institutional marxist, and still less does it lend itself to the kind of intellectual somersaults which often go with academic marxism like that of E.J. Hobsbawm. And yet, when it comes to career advancement in the academic world and fame in the British intellectual community, clever mental gymnastics seem to carry more weight than Ostergaard's moral staunchness. Clearly Ostergaard had a severe handicap amongst the armchair academics in the back-biting atmosphere of the university establishment, and amidst students who, as Wittgenstein complained, merely demand 'formulas', like marxism, to project themselves through their exams without having to think too much.

Geoffrey Ostergaard lacked the dazzle of an intellectual juggler like Hobsbawm: the trendier debates on the English Standard of Living in the Nineteenth Century, the Labour Aristocracy, Methodism and the Elie Halevy thesis, Bandits and Primitive Rebels were not part of Geoffrey's repertoire. Ostergaard studied at Oxford under the socialist scholar and former Guild Socialist G.D.H. Cole, and developed his research in the rather staid, straightforward narrative and chronological history of the British labour movement. His work was less than exotic and had a flavour of the mundane: from a thesis entitled *Public Ownership in Great Britain* in 1953 he went on to produce publications like *Co-operative Democracy* (1955), *Constitutional Relations Between Co-operatives and Labour Parties* (1960), *Power in Co-operatives* (1965). His approach was that of a dry steadfast chronicler of events.

Later came his work on India and non-violence: *Gandhian Non-violence* (1978) and *Resisting the Nation State* (1982), together with what has been described as two authoritative books *The Gentle Anarchists* (1971) with Melville Currell and *Non-Violent Revolution in India* (1985).

Managerialist Party and the International Bankers

Here we are concerned with Ostergaard's middle period. That is that part of his work produced in the 1950s and '60s for *Freedom*, *Anarchy* and given at occasional anarchist Summer Schools. This work relates to his analysis of the trade unions, anarcho-syndicalism, the Labour Party, the British Labour Movement, Fabianism and managerialism. Perhaps his most substantial contribution, written in the narrative style, is his thirteen-part piece entitled *The Tradition of Workers' Control*. This is an uneasy journey starting with Robert Owen and the Grand National Consolidated Trade Union of 1834, with its early conceptions of community and worker control, only to end up with the 1945-51 Labour Government and nationalisation devised by Herbert Morrison and Lord Citrine on the basis of what Ostergaard calls "managerial socialism" through the state administration of certain public corporations. The history of an idea transmogrified in the modern mind and finally presided over by the new managerial classes to become the glorious 'Theatre of the Absurd' that nationalisation became. A theory of public ownership to "secure for the workers by hand or by brain the full fruits of their industry" in the terms of the old Clause Four, became the excuse for what the syndicalists of the old Syndicalist Workers' Federation called 'the New Boss Class' in a new managerialist state.

It is Ostergaard's exposure of the managerial nature of the Labour Party which, for me, is most revealing. In his essay *Fabian and Parliamentary Socialism* (1962) he insists: "The Labour leadership made it quite clear – that by socialism it understood, not a new social order but regulated Welfare State capitalism". A more detailed account of the deep faith in leaders, professionals and experts of every description, which many members and factions of the Labour Party seem to have, is contained in his *Fabianism and the Managerial Revolution* (1954). The Fabians and the Fabian Society have had a lasting ideological influence on the Labour Party and were prominent in devising the old Clause Four in 1918. The Fabians, Ostergaard shows us, are modernists and just as much as Henry Ford are obsessed with the economies of scale, especially after 1918, when their emphasis on political bureaucracy declined, to be replaced by "a growing emphasis on the importance of the managerial elements in a socialist society".

In one of Ostergaard's most telling paragraphs he declares: "When the future historian comes to write the history of the managerial social revolution in this country, he will undoubtedly assign a prime role to the Fabians. To them belongs the credit for preparing the way for the peaceful emergence of the *new ruling class* by the elaboration of a 'socialist' ideology which could, at one and the same time, enlist the sympathy of the proletariat without antagonising those *elements of the old capitalist class which were to be enrolled in the new ruling class of managers."*

This process will continue under Mr Blair's Clause Four of 1995. The Labour Party, despite the trade unions whose role is now in decline, will remain a party dedicated to a notion of salvation through management and planning by 'experts'. The state socialist confusion, which Ostergaard mentions, that state control somehow means community control will go on.

In a way, as Ostergaard implies, the Labour Party as the party of planning has been the agent of management and trade unions in the same way as the Conservative Party has been the party of business and the City. Managerialism and syndicalism, bossism and workerism, have been the truculent twins of this the 'People's Party'. The reason for this managerial element in British State Socialism is, as Ostergaard shows, largely thanks to the Fabian Society. The early Fabians, it is true, had a large number of upper civil servants who stressed the importance of 'efficient bureaucratic administration'. But after 1918, Ostergaard says, the emphasis on political bureaucracy disappears to be replaced by more stress on the managerial elements. With this high regard for both bureaucratic and managerial administration went the notion that political power was not for 'ordinary mortals' but best in the hands of the 'super-intelligent administrator' eager to commit acts of social engineering.

In his essay *Industry and the Managerial Society* (1957) Ostergaard says: "The sad truth of the matter is that the Labour Party cannot be expected to formulate any measures to prevent the emergence of a managerial order. Of the two major parties in this country, its attitude towards the managers is more ambivalent and on the whole more favourable than that of the Conservative Party which, broadly speaking, still represents capitalist interests."

Of course there is a tussle between managerialism and syndicalism within the Labour Party, but, as Ostergaard shows, "there are too many men of power in the Labour Party and the trade union hierarchy with an actual or potential interest in managerialism". And in the same essay he warns that "the political elite and the managerial elite are merging".

Despite this seizure of control by the managerial castes within the Labour Party, unity has been retained for three-quarters of a century by Clause Four and its promise of nationalisation. Clause Four allowed labourite social reformers and socialists to co-exist uneasily within the same party. The re-wording of Clause Four from a vague class struggle tract to a moralistic play-on-words in the new Clause Four of 1995, will still leave the manager and social engineer in the driving seat. It all reflects a kind of derelict liberalism, an appeal to what Malcolm Muggeridge (*Chronicles of Wasted Time*, 1982) contemptuously called "moderate men of all shades of opinion" to produce a party committed to modest progress, within the limits of the law.

In his recent book *Remaking the Labour Party: from Gaitskell to Blair* (1996) Tudor Jones says: "In the past, Labour's socialist myth – of a new social order founded on public ownership of the means of production – had helped imbue the Party's members and supporters with a spirit of collective identity and common endeavour and purpose ... It had offered them the goal of conquering the commanding heights of the economy, the necessary stage to the socialist commonwealth." Mr Jones wonders if the glue of Tony Blair's 'communitarian core vision' – a kind of abstract fantasy – will replace the idea of public ownership as another socialist 'touchstone' in the global market economy.

Ostergaard was clearly right to focus on the rise of managerialism both in the Labour Party and the modern world. In 1947 George Orwell had said as much in a review called 'Burnham's View of the Contemporary World Struggle': "*The Managerial Revolution* [by James Burnham], for instance, seems to me a good description of what is actually happening in various parts of the world, i.e. the growth of societies neither capitalist nor socialist, and organised more or less on the lines of a caste system."

But Ostergaard may have been a bit too narrowly engaged on the then fashionable academic theory of managerialism. Many socialists, and particularly Fabians, as he says may not have been 'on the make' (see *Socialism by Pressure Group*, 1961), and yet parliamentary socialism because of the nature of international finance was bound to fail. The capitalist dimension cannot be overlooked. When Malcolm Muggeridge described the downfall of the second Labour government, he said Ramsay MacDonald and the rest of the Labour Cabinet gathered in the back garden at 10 Downing Street to await a call from the New York banking houses about a loan to let the Treasury keep the pound on the gold standard. When the answer came as 'no', MacDonald was left to go to the Palace and resign.

To Muggeridge this incident finished off any notion that "the Labour Party, or any Social Democratic party similarly constituted, can be an effective instrument of fundamental social change". And he went on to declare: "Whenever, subsequently, I read or heard prospectuses of the great things a Labour government might be expected to achieve, I remember that little cluster of respectable-looking men in the garden at 10 Downing Street, drawing at their pipes, occasionally getting up to stretch their legs, while they waited for Wall Street to decide their fate."

Despite the march of modernism and the rise of managerialism, international capitalism will still have a role in the survival of the next Labour government.

Syndicalism: political nonentity, workplace reality

The dilemma for the radical who, like Ostergaard, wants to go to the root of the social crisis of our time, beyond political reform and cosmetic surgery, is that most people are focused on and agitated by local and immediate issues and problems. Rarely do they spare a thought for the structure of the huge system of finance and power which torments them. And if they did think about things like state capitalism or corporate managerial frameworks in society, they would see it like the weather, unpleasant but an inevitable consequence of things beyond their control.

Most of the passions and resentments of the English workman are directed against the boss and the management, and those things which impinge directly upon him and his family. As a young apprentice I was always struck by the widespread conviction on the shopfloor of managerial incompetence. How ironic then that the party which goes under the name Labour Party should, as Ostergaard shows, have so much faith in management.

But this kind of hole-in-corner syndicalism, this shopfloor syndicalism, syndicalism of the workplace, is a long way from what Ostergaard calls "the class war" heroically "to be fought to a victorious finish with no compromise given or taken" (see *The Relevance of Syndicalism* in *Anarchy 28*). The idea of 'no class collaboration' is an absurd Sorelian myth for scabby-arsed sectarians. Anyone who has been a shop steward in negotiations with middle management knows that they are characterised by appeals to give-and-take, reciprocity and fair play. As the sociologist William Baldamus pointed out (*Efficiency and Effort: an analysis of industrial administration*, 1961), such confrontations end up quantifying moral considerations such as issues of 'fairness' rather than the level of company dividends or the productivity of the workforce.

In the 1960s the idea of managerialism, which Ostergaard took up, was academically fashionable, but his ideological response in anarcho-syndicalism or syndicalism was, as he admitted (see 'The Relevance of Syndicalism' in *Anarchy 28*), almost to invite the label of 'crank'. Management and the 'manufacture of consent' under the factory regime is now seen as vital to the study of what is called the 'Labour Process'. It may be that reluctance to discuss big company dividends in pay negotiations is part of what Michael Burawoy (see *Manufacturing Consent: Changes in the Labour Process under Monopoly Capitalism*, 1979) describes as "simultaneous obscuring and securing of surplus value". It could equally be, as one bunch of middle managers told me, that many managers don't understand dividends any more than their workers do.

Geoffrey Ostergaard was a pragmatic anarcho-syndicalist: in 1957, in an article entitled 'Anarchy and Trade Unionism' (reprinted in *Anarchy 40*), he suggested "the time is not propitious" to create anarcho-syndicalist trade unions, but later in *Anarchy*, June 1963, following the dramatic Spies for Peace incident and a revival of interest in anarchism in Britain, Ostergaard declared: "It is ... no extravagance to claim that the spirit of syndicalism ... is once again in the air".

What is extraordinary about this is not that syndicalism seemed to revive, but that it should ever have been regarded as "dormant ... in this country". It has been a virtual political non-entity, while in the workplace it has continued to be an everyday reality. This has been illustrated in the development of industrial sociology more recently. But the evidence of the case for shopfloor syndicalism was here before, as the industrial sociologist Paul Thompson shows: "Goodrich's classic 1920 study of workshop politics (*The Frontier of Control*) showed how workers countered managerial power by extending their own 'frontiers of control' with respect to organisation of work, changes in technology and methods of payment. Demands for workers' control were an extension of the degree of job control already exercised"(*The Nature of Work*, 1989).

Perhaps the reason that syndicalism continued to have an underground and almost unofficial existence on the shopfloor in this country, and only occasionally became politically centre stage, has to do with the fact, as Thompson says, "official socialist movements showed little interest and sometimes active hostility" to the politics of production and the daily struggles inside the factory regimes. Even most of the British anarchists have historically remained aloof from shopfloor struggles, leaving intervention to small numbers of anarcho-syndicalists and 'revolutionary syndicalists'.

On this issue Ostergaard (*Industry and the Managerial Society*, 1957) quoted Malatesta approvingly: "The error of having abandoned the Labour movement has done an immense injury to anarchism, but at least it leaves unaltered the distinctive character. The error of confounding the anarchist movement with trade unionism would be still more grave."

Only in Spain did the anarchist movement launch a full-scale commitment to the struggles of the labour movement with the consequences we now know well. Even as I write, the Spanish press is reporting industrial riots in Puerto Real, Cadiz and Seville among workers in the shipbuilding and repair yards protesting at government attempts to reorganise their industry. Anarcho-syndicalist unions like the CNT (Confederación Naciónal de Trabajadores) and CGT have a long tradition of radical action in these areas and industries. Perhaps the smaller scale nature of Spanish industry, with the background of artisan tradition and a huge rural and peasant base on which to draw, made the Spanish trade unions a more comfortable place for anarchists to work. More comfortable than the entrenched massive factory regimes of Germany and Britain.

The public face of syndicalism in Britain has been like taking a history ride on Blackpool's Big Dipper. Both Ostergaard in his *The Tradition of Workers' Control*, and G.D.H. Cole in *A Short History of the British Working Class Movement 1787-1947*, present the course of trade unionism and direct action as a series of peaks and troughs. The ups and downs of syndicalism and proto-syndicalist movements from the industrial revolution onwards. From the primitive and heroic beginnings with machine breakers and Grand National Consolidated Trades Union in the first half of the nineteenth century; 1850 brought a more legalistic approach with the conservative 'New Model' unions of the engineers and the cotton operatives. Later, between 1900 and 1914, came what Ostergaard calls "the classic syndicalist movement", and to it and Guild Socialism he devotes the lion's share of his history of *The Tradition of Workers' Control*. Up to 1910, though syndicalism was a recognisable entity, Bob Holton (see *British Syndicalism 1900-1914*) says it could be dismissed as a propagandist movement; with the revival of industrial unrest between 1910 and 1914 it took on a more significant character. After the General Strike of 1926, syndicalism was out of the picture until perhaps its final fling in the 1970s when, during the strikes of that decade, forms of workers' control and workers' councils were again given some consideration. Probably its political swan-song was the collapse of the miners' strike in 1984-85.

Although Ostergaard had predicted this final surge of syndicalism in the early 1960s, he had shifted the focus of his research from British anarcho-syndicalism to Indian pacifism before it had begun to become a reality. Signs of the re-emergence of syndicalism as a political force were already there in 1963, when Ostergaard made his claim in *The Relevance of Syndicalism*, and by the 1970s far from being a social crank or 'troglodyte' he would have been in the mainstream.

In 1960 some anarchists, syndicalists and radical socialists tried to launch the National Rank and File Movement. This was a reflection of the times and by the middle of the 1960s the unofficial strike rate was so high in Britain as to justify a Royal Commission, which produced the Donovan Report (1968). In France in 1968, and Italy in 1969, an even higher level of industrial and social conflict was reached during massive strike waves. But the demands often went beyond wages to struggles over authority relations in the factory, control over the line speeds and piece work, questioning of job hierarchies and staff upgradings, etc. As K. Kumar (*Prophecy and Progress*, 1978) observed: "The changing pattern of strikes, especially since 1945, gives further evidence of an increasing restlessness about the quality of working life and the nature of the job itself".

The snag was that this blast of radical large-scale trade union activity in Britain lacked an anarchist or anarcho-syndicalist influence. Malatesta, and later Ostergaard, may have been right to advise the anarchist movement to steer clear of deep involvement in the unions, but the British Labour Movement has suffered from this lack of a libertarian input. It produced short-sighted trade unions, mindless militants and union bosses willing to collaborate with the state and employers, and when it did become radical, as in the miners' strikes of 1984-85, leaders like Arthur Scargill emerge; men without a serious strategy for changing society.

John McIlroy, in his book *Trade Unions in Britain Today* (1988), says: "The idea of *semi-syndicalist* ... trade unionism has been best exemplified in the 1980s by Arthur Scargill and the NUM". McIlroy claims 'semi-syndicalist unionism' doesn't accept the standard British trade union distinction between 'the industrial' and 'the political' action. Scargill, and what McIlroy calls the 'semi-syndicalists', seemed to believe that though the industrial muscle of the miners' strike in 1984 a political transformation could come about. He was, and is, a skilful tactician on the industrial battlefield, but a hopeless incompetent when it came to winning the war in society. More recently McIlroy complains of Scargill's lack of a developed political grasp, another aspect of crude 'semi-syndicalism'. But anarchists would probably point to the lack of vision and a social perspective in Scargill – an absence of a convincingly coherent strategy – in a politically sceptical British society.

The reason the anarchists have mostly held aloof from labour and the workplace may have something to do with the intellectual and sectarian ghettos they tend historically to occupy in this country. In the early 1960s, when Ostergaard was writing, they were forced out of these ghettos by the rapid growth of the Campaign for Nuclear Disarmament and the peace movement, as E.J. Hobsbawm noted (*Labouring Men*, 1968): "... the implicitly pacifist Campaign for Nuclear Disarmament, which has not merely become the most massive anti-nuclear movement in the world ... and a model for (less successful) foreign imitators, but a major force in British politics outside its narrow terms of reference". The result was that the British anarchists experienced something of a renaissance.

This all had some consequence for anarcho-syndicalist involvement in industry during the decade, as Ostergaard soon detected, of which the formation of the National Rank and File Movement was the earliest example. Unfortunately this did not continue into the 1970s. By then many of the mature militants had been lost or distracted, or were burnt out.

The experienced building workers, print workers, engineers and dockers evaporated from the 'libertarian' ranks through the 1960s. Brian Behan (building trade) drifted away early on; Bill Christopher (print) left Freedom Press to rejoin the Independent Labour Party in the late 1960s; Jack Stevenson dropped out; Peter Turner, a joiner and active trade unionist, remained at Freedom Press but was deeply occupied in editorial activities; James Pinkerton (print) resigned as secretary of the Syndicalist Workers' Federation in 1963; Ken Hawkes (journalist) and Tom Brown (engineering) both retired from active syndicalism by the end of the decade. Many of the younger end hadn't much trade union experience, and for some anarcho-syndicalism was just another label, while for most the Vietnam War became their obsession.

Is it not ironic that when Ostergaard's forecast of the 'relevance of syndicalism' came to the forefront of British political life, as it did in the 1970s, the British anarchist movement was so ill-equipped to respond? It was as if the anarchists wanted the peace movement and the 1960s to continue forever, at a time when industrial unrest was widespread and trade unions more openly militant. Writers like Burawoy, Donald Roy[1] in the USA and Hugh Benyon[2] here, by focusing on shopfloor culture were confirming a tradition of syndicalism in which workers, at the point of production, continually tried to snatch control from management.

The anarchists and anarcho-syndicalists failed to see the significance of the changes, and switch their struggle from direct action in the streets against the Vietnam War and the Bomb, to the factories and picket lines at the end of the 1960s. Instead of lots of small unofficial strikes as in the early 1960s, the 1970s brought more big official strikes backed by the unions. In the north of England, the small Manchester group of International Socialists (later the SWP) – led by two young sociologists, Colin Barker and John Lee – supported the strikers at Roberts-Arundel, Stockport, in their marathon year-long dispute. The larger Manchester Anarchist Group stayed out of the strike and suffered as a result. Later there was little anarchist involvement in the Pilkington glassworkers strike at St Helens, which turned into a strike against the workers' union – the General and Municipal Workers' Union, led by Lord Cooper – as much as against the employer.

The Pilkington strike shook the trade union movement, and big unions like the engineers (AEU) and the Transport and General

---

1. *Working for Ford* by H. Benyon (1973).

2. *Banana Time, Job Satisfaction and Informal Interaction* by D.F. Roy (1973); *Fear Stuff, Sweet Stuff and Evil Stuff: management defences against unionisation in the South* by D.F. Roy (1980).

Workers' Union became more ready to declare strikes official. Factory occupations and the take-over by Upper Clyde Shipbuilders of their yard followed. Then there was the miners' strike and the three-day week, and the fall of Ted Heath's Tory government.

Most anarchists, and so-called syndicalists, seemed untouched by these syndicalist developments. The Vietnam War was more remarkable than St Helens and the Upper Clyde. The Angry Brigade in the UK, the Baader-Meinhof Gang in West Germany, the Italian Red Brigade and the plight of Spanish political prisoners proved more thrilling for most libertarians than our own native dockers, shipyard workers, mechanics, engineers and glassworkers. A world of passports and clandestine endeavours charmed us more than the daily grind of clocking-on and clocking-off. Peter Turner and Bill Christopher, through *Freedom*, tried to cover the industrial scene. There was some involvement in small disputes such as Dunlop at Rochdale in 1969 where an anarchist shop steward was victimised. In the early 1970s anarcho-syndicalists became involved in some Asian workers' strikes in Lancashire at the Courtaulds company. This was followed by an anarcho-syndicalist campaign for shop stewards in the textile industry in some North West towns. But these were small, isolated libertarian interventions onto Britain's industrial scene.

Perhaps the anarchists and younger syndicalists feared the anti-intellectualism for which the British labour movement is famous. But as Hobsbawm says, the Hispanic countries often blended anti-intellectualism "with anarchist traditions of direct action". There must be other reasons. Intellectual and sectarian politics often makes for an easier life, without the rough and tumble trade union activities. This sectarianism without sacrifice led to a dispute between shopfloor syndicalists and sectarian syndicalists in the Syndicalist Workers' Federation in the mid-1970s.

Inexperience and narrow intellectual sectarianism are two explanations why anarchists and anarcho-syndicalists failed to take advantage of this upsurge of public syndicalism. Outside factories many of them were unaware of the unpublicised undercurrent of syndicalism in British industry, before it was uncovered by the Donovan Report on Trade Unions and Employers' Associations (1968) and by the industrial sociologists. Even the academic historian Ostergaard, highly regarded by some syndicalists, and the working class folksy historian of the SWF Tom Brown, seem only to have a vague grasp of the battles for control of the factory regimes.

Romanticism was another thing which plagued us at that time. Stuart Christie had been released from his Spanish jail in 1967 and written of his plot to kill Franco in *The News of the World*. The French uprising of 1968 had culminated with the workers rejecting the fraternisation of the students. There were riotous demonstrations in London against the US involvement in the Vietnam war. The Angry Brigade made its debut; bombs against the Franco regime were planted at a London branch of the Banco de Bilbao.

Charisma triumphed at a time when, in Britain at least, the humdrum was required. Flower power and exotic campaigns to outrage became preferred to the everyday struggles of factory workers. The writings of Geoffrey Ostergaard, at that time in the 1970s so significant to the lives of the British public and their industrial struggles, were forgotten or ignored in the great welter of fanciful exploits. Neither flower power or the Angry Brigade offered any serious alternative, but some project based on Ostergaard's ideas of anarcho-syndicalism could have come up with something plausible. In 1954 he claimed: "... syndicalism of the period 1900-1920 now appears as the great heroic movement of the proletariat, the last desperate attempt before society took the plunge down the managerial abyss ... to build up a distinctive proletarian culture ... and evolve a uniquely proletarian method on social action". The period between 1970 and 1984 represented another chance to put the brake on the managerial nightmare, and illustrated the intellectual bankruptcy of the political left in Britain.

Brian Bamford

The Tradition of Workers' Control

In this essay I shall attempt to do three things: first to sketch in outline the development of the concept of Workers' Control in this country; secondly, on the basis of this historical sketch, to clarify and to assess the significance of the concept; and thirdly, to advance a number of possible explanations of why, both in theory and in practice, the idea has met with such little success.

The phrase, 'Workers' Control of Industry', was first coined by the Guild Socialists in the years immediately prior to the First World War but the idea behind it can be traced back to the origin of the socialist movement in this country. The socialist movement itself was a reaction on the part of sections of the working class to conditions created by the Industrial Revolution of the eighteenth century. One of the central features of this revolution was the transformation of the productive system: the 'domestic system' of industry was replaced by the 'factory system' and the independent craftsman, owning his own tools and living by the sale of the products of his work, increasingly gave way to the industrial proletarian, owning little or nothing but his labour power which, in order to subsist, he was compelled to sell, on whatever terms he could get, to the capitalist owners of the new factories. Today, we are so accustomed to this method of production and its concomitant, the wage system, that it requires an effort of imagination to appreciate the significance of the change in terms of the lives of ordinary workers. From being, within limits, an independent craftsman or peasant with an assured place in his local community, the worker became, in the eyes of the masters of the new economic system, a mere commodity – a unit of labour, subject, as were all commodities, to the inexorable laws of the market. In a word, the worker became *alienated* not only from the means of production and the products of his labour but also from the community.

In these circumstances, it is not surprising to find that the new socialist theories proposed an alternative to the capitalist system which would avoid this alienation of the vast majority of the people. This alternative was the autonomous, self-supporting communist community – what Robert Owen called the Village of Co-operation. In each of these villages, which were to be federated for purposes of mutual aid, it was proposed that some 2,000 individuals on the same number of acres of land should combine the pursuits of industry and agriculture, share all things in common, and reap collectively the full fruits of their labour.

For a whole generation this community idea dominated the minds of socialists and co-operators – the terms were practically synonymous – and several abortive attempts were made to implement it. The reasons for the failure of the community experiments and the virtual abandonment of the idea after 1850 would lead us too far afield. Suffice it to say that one of the reasons for the eclipse of the idea, quite apart from the inevitable reaction to practical failure, was the growing feeling on the part of many workers that it was no longer necessary to create a community *outside* the confines of existing society. The workers were capable of winning political and social rights *within* the existing social framework and could thus repair the breach wrought by their alienation from the local community of the first generations of industrial proletarians. Henceforth, socialists tended to concentrate their attention on the hub of the social system – the mode of production.

Even before the community movement had exhausted itself, there had been a move in this direction. In the late 1820s, alongside the co-operative stores which had been set up to accumulate the collective capital to start a community, there had arisen a number of 'union' shops sponsored by Owenite trade unionists. In these 'union' shops, groups of workers, usually in the same trade and prompted by strikes or lock-outs, had in effect established a system of co-operative self-employment. By a natural process, these activities gave rise to a number of Exchange Bazaars of which the one opened by Owen in Gray's lnn Road, 1832, was only the most famous. Using labour notes expressed in hours of labour time, the Bazaars sought to arrange the exchange of the products of one particular trade for those of others.

'A Different State of Things'

These first halting attempts to establish a rudimentary co-operative economic system were, however, soon overshadowed by a new movement among trade unionists. Inspired by the relative success of the 'union' shops and the growing strength of the trade unions, Owen became convinced that his ideas could be applied in a new way. Let the workers, he said, unite in one great union, divided into departments according to their various trades, and they can then take over the whole industry of the country. It was with this ultimate object that the famous Grand National Consolidated Trades Union of 1834 was formed. The two-fold purpose of syndicalist unions – the protection of the workers under the existing system and the formation of the nuclei of the future society – is evident in Rule XLVI of the Grand National: "That, although the design of the Union is, in the first instance, to raise the wages of the workmen, or prevent any further reduction therein, and to diminish the hours of labour, the great and ultimate object of it must be to establish the paramount rights of Industry and Humanity, by instituting such measures as shall effectually prevent the ignorant, idle and useless part of society from having undue control over the fruits of our toil, which, through the agency of the vicious money system, they at present possess; and that, consequently, the Unionists should lose no opportunity of mutually encouraging and assisting each other in bringing about A DIFFERENT STATE OF THINGS, in which the really useful and intelligent part of society only shall have the direction of its affairs, and in which well-directed industry and virtue shall meet their just distinction and reward, and vicious idleness its merited contempt and destitution."

The dramatic collapse of the Grand National later in the same year scotched for a time the notion of a revolutionary transformation of society and in the years that followed the energies of the workers were largely diverted into three channels: (i) the Chartist movement, aiming at political reform; (ii) the 'new model' trade union movement, which sought to organise and to improve the lot of skilled workers within the existing capitalist framework; and (iii) the distributive co-operative movement, which sought to benefit its members through a system of mutual trading in which the profits were returned to the customers. The notion of workers jointly owning their own workshops and thereby securing the full fruits of their labour did not, however, die. In 1845 John Drury, a Sheffield trade unionist, was instrumental in forming the National Association of United Trades for the Employment of Labour with the object of raising capital with which to employ men who were on strikes approved by the sister Organisation, the NA of UT for the Protection of Labour. And, in the following year, a group of Owenites and others started a number of Redemption Societies which proposed to seek 'the redemption of labour' by using the subscriptions of its members to establish self-governing workshops and land settlements.

A more substantial expression of the same idea was found in the activities of the Christian Socialists between 1848 and 1854. J.M. Ludlow and his colleagues were originally inspired not by their Owenite predecessors but by the French disciples of Saint-Simon, P.J. Buchez and Louis Blanc. Condemning the wage-system as a 'sort of washed-out slavery', they saw producers' co-operation as 'the practical application of Christianity to the purposes of trade and industry'.

'Direct Association for Production'

The Society for Promoting Working Men's Associations – the Christian Socialist organisation – was responsible for initiating a number of self-governing workshops in the tailoring, baking, building, and shoe-making trades. In themselves, these short-lived associations could do little to stem the tide of commercial competition. Indeed, they sometimes found themselves competing against each other. To obviate this, Vansittart Neale proposed to unite all the associates in a particular trade into one Association. This proposal was rejected by the men themselves but the direction of thought implied in it led to the ideal of linking the associations with the trade unions. In a circular to all trade unions, Neale urged them 'to substitute for a mere defensive organisation the application of the principle of direct labour for production, distribution and consumption' and made certain concrete proposals: that in each trade a Model Association should be set up for employing out of work members and that in the localities a number of different trade societies should combine to establish Co-operative Stores to supply articles of domestic consumption, raw materials for the productive associations, and a market for these associations, the outlay being met by special working class journals and in September 1851 the newly-formed Amalgamated Society of Engineers announced a plan for taking over the Windsor Ironworks at Liverpool. Unfortunately, before sufficient capital could be raised, there occurred the famous lock-out of the engineers in the Spring of 1852 which used up all the Union's surplus funds.

After the breakdown of this plan, the Christian Socialist movement began to wane. One by one the associations broke up. Trouble frequently arose between the managers, responsible to the Promoters, and the associates who wanted to be completely self-governing at once; and disputes over the method of apportioning the surplus were long and, at times, bitter. Concluding that 'working men were not fit for association', most of the Christian Socialist leaders turned their attention to the cause of working class education, and the new movement came to an end. In the light of history, however, the movement is interesting not so much for its failure to achieve permanent results as for the fact that, starting from different premises, animated by different motives, and largely ignorant of what had happened in the early 1830s, the Christian Socialists had eventually arrived in their organisational ideas at something closely resembling that of the Owenite trade unionists – despite their rejection of the revolutionary approach.

The one Christian Socialist who remained active in the working class movement was Neale. In the decades that followed, he and men like the old Owenite missionary, George Jacob Holyoake, kept alive the idea of producers' co-operation. In the sixties and seventies, mainly in the North of England and in Scotland, there were various practical attempts to revive the ideal with only limited, short-term success. By this time most of the trade unions, with the notable exception of those in the mining industry, had settled down to the job of working the wage-system and Co-operation and Trade Unionism tended to drift apart and to pursue their different courses independently. Ironically enough, it was left to the then fashionable liberal economist, John Stuart Mill, rather than to the leaders of the trade union 'Junta', to envisage the supersession of the wage-system. In a passage which shocked his orthodox readers, he predicted:

"The form of association ... which if mankind continue to improve, must be expected in the end to predominate, is not that which can exist between a capitalist as chief and work people without a voice in management, but the association of the labourers themselves on terms of equality, collectively owning the capital with which they carry on their operations working under managers elected and removable by themselves."

Producers' versus Consumers' Co-operation

Meanwhile, the distributive Co-operative Movement had been making steady progress and in 1867 was in a position to establish on a firm foundation a federal Wholesale Society. In 1872 the CWS embarked on its first productive venture and in so doing touched off a fierce controversy in the movement. The issue was this: When Co-operation extends to production, who should control, the consumers or the producers? To most of the old Co-operative pioneers there was no doubt about the answer. In production, the producers should control and anything else was a perpetuation of the wage-system. In the event, however, it was the protagonists of the consumer, the self-styled 'practical men' who controlled the wholesale and retail societies, who won the day. With the specious argument that the consumer represented a universal interest whereas the producer represented only a sectional interest, they enrolled themselves in the ranks of their ostensible opponents – the class which employed wage labour. Nobody who today reads the debates which accompanied this fateful step can but sense the guilty conscience of the consumer advocates or fail to notice the evident sigh of relief when, in 1891, the respectable Miss Potter, shortly to become Mrs Sidney Webb, published her famous book on the Co-operative Movement in which she, in effect, damned producer co-operatives as associations of little capitalists. Henceforth, the consumers could draw their dividends with a good heart, secure in the knowledge that consumer control was in conformity with the views of the pundits of Fabian socialism!

The champions of the producer within the Co-operative Movement did not, of course, quit the field. On the contrary, they redoubled their efforts and in the closing decades of the nineteenth century succeeded in establishing a permanent foothold. In the process, however, and partly in response to the challenge of the consumer advocates, they modified their original ideas. For the purely self-governing workshop, they substituted the idea of a co-partnership between the providers of capital, the consumers and the workers. Henceforth, co-operative co-partnerships were to be composed of shareholding members, each with one vote, who might be either workers in the enterprise, retail or other productive societies, trade unions, or interested individuals, mainly ex-workers. Any surplus was to be divided between the three elements of the co-partnership in the forms of a fixed or maximum return to capital, a dividend to customers, and a bonus to workers in proportion to wages. Management was to be vested in a committee elected by the members but no society could qualify as a genuine co-partnership unless the workers in the enterprise participated directly in its control.

Today, there are some forty-odd co-operative co-partnerships organised on these principles, most of them linked to a federal organisation, the Co-operative Productive Federation, founded in 1882. Confined mainly to the clothing, boot and shoe, printing and building trades – all of which require a relatively small amount of working capital – and trading almost exclusively with the retail co-operative movement, these societies have managed to survive in an economic climate which has become increasingly hostile to the fundamental principles. Whatever their defects, both in theory and practice, they remain the clearest examples of practical workers' control in this country. By their very existence they refute the wild generalisation that ordinary working men and women are incapable of controlling industrial undertakings.

The Forerunners of Syndicalism

In following the trend of thought which has led to Co-operative Co-partnerships, I have necessarily by-passed other manifestations of the idea of workers' control. For reasons which are partly to be explained by the peculiar insularity of the Co-operative Movement and partly by an unfortunate association in earlier years with so-called capitalist co-partnership and profit-sharing, the protagonists of co-operative co-partnership have never had much impact on the thought of the rest of the socialist movement. The advocates of workers' control to whom I now turn have been, for the most part, either unaware of their existence and thus ignorant of the lessons it teaches or unconvinced by its claims that, by peaceful means, it could transform the capitalist system.

To pick up the thread of the story, it is necessary to recall that, until the 1880s with the minor exception of a few of the later Chartists, socialism in England meant essentially voluntary socialism as exemplified in the Co-operative Movement. The so-called 'socialist revival' of the 1880s was in fact an importation into this country of foreign, mainly Continental State Socialist, ideas – plus the alleged 'discovery' by the Fabians that state intervention was socialism in disguise! Of the three schools of socialist thought which had become established by the end of the 1880s – the Marxist, the Fabian-Labour and the anti-State or Anarchist – only the latter, it need hardly be said, was at all favourably disposed to the idea of workers' control. Out-Marxing Marx himself, Hyndman and the SDF stood for the simple 'nationalisation formula' – the nationalisation of the means of production, distribution and exchange – and facilely argued that this was the solution to all problems. The Fabians, more cautiously, stood for 'the emancipation of Land and Industrial Capital from individual and class ownership'. More to the point, they persuaded themselves and most of their labour listeners that socialism implied consumer sovereignty and that the state was nothing but a glorified consumer co-op! Self-appointed apostles of the coming Collective State, they roundly denounced all who wished to abolish the wage-system. Not its abolition but its nationalisation was what they demanded.

In a particularly revealing essay on 'The Illusions of Socialism' Shaw put the point thus. Contrasting the enthusiasts, who conceive the idea of socialism and who win converts to their ideals by presenting civilisation as a popular melodrama, with the statesmen who in the 'raw reality' have to draw up concrete proposals, capable of being adopted by a real government and carried out by a real executive, Shaw stated: "Out of the illusion of 'the abolition of the wage system' we shall get steady wages for everybody and finally discredit all other sources of income as disreputable. By the illusion of the downfall of Capitalism we shall turn whole nations into Joint Stock Companies; and our determination to annihilate the bourgeoisie will end in making every workman a bourgeois gentilhomme. By the illusion of Democracy, or government by everybody, we shall establish the most powerful bureaucracy ever known on the face of the earth, and finally get rid of popular election, trial by jury, and all the other makeshifts of a system in which no man can be trusted with power ..."[1]

The Socialist League

Not all Fabians were as frank or perhaps as prescient as Shaw but it is not difficult to understand why the freedom-loving William Morris reacted so violently against collectivist socialism. Roundly asserting that "individual men cannot shuffle off the business of life on to the shoulders of an abstraction called the State, but must deal with it in conscious association with each other", Morris and his colleagues in the Socialist League (1885-1894) looked forward to the establishment of socialism by means of free associations. At this time many in the libertarian socialist and anarchist camps – notably Kropotkin – were sceptical of the possibility of winning over the trade unions to their cause, but a section were more hopeful. Two of the earliest publications of the League were in fact expressly addressed to trade unionists. One, by Belfort Bax, urged all unionists "to unite themselves with a view, at the earliest possible date, of laying hands on the means of production, distribution and exchange" and "to direct their energies towards consolidating and federating with the distinct end of constituting themselves the nucleus of the socialist commonwealth".[2] The other, by Thomas Binning, in a similar vein, argued that the unions "contain within themselves all the elements essential for the constitution of a rational society; they are therefore pointed out as the natural pioneers of the New Era".[3] A few years later the anarchists of the *Freedom* group expressed the same conviction that the trade unions could do much to lay the foundations of the free society. In an important article, 'What's to be done', in *Freedom*, February 1892, a contributor argued that "Unions are free spontaneous associations of working men waiting to do anarchistic work". Their great fault, he continued, lay in their preoccupation with mere defence and their too narrow ideal. They must be made to realise that "if the worker is to be a free man he must be a joint owner with his fellows of the means of production, and that to obtain the control of these is the end and aim of the labour movement". When trade unionists have become inspired with the ideal of being their own employers, their own masters, then, he continued, the future social revolution will be an anarchist revolution and its motto will be: 'The land to the labourer, the mine to the miner, the tool to the toiler, the produce to the producer'.

I have introduced these quotations not because the Socialist League and the *Freedom* group were influential – although their influence has been consistently underestimated by Fabian historians – but because they provide part of the evidence for the view that syndicalist aspirations, in one form or another, have formed a continuous tradition on the part of at least a minority of British workers. To many observers, the classical syndicalist movement of the period 1910-20 was as exotic in character as its name. In truth, however, most of the basic ideas of the movement can be found in the earlier publications of the Socialist League and in *Freedom*. By the 1890s the Fabian-Labour tide in British socialism was rising fast but there remained a current of thought hostile to the new collectivism. Even the Webbs in their *History of Trade Unionism* were forced to admit that "there always remained, in the hearts of the manual working class of Great Britain, an instinctive faith in the ... idea of Associations of Producers owning as such both the instruments and the products of their labour".[4] Without this 'instinctive faith' and the propaganda of the anarchists and libertarian socialists, it is doubtful whether the later syndicalist movement would have flourished as it did.

British Syndicalism

Although it is true that most of the ideas of the classical syndicalist movement had been anticipated, there was something really distinctive about the new movement: its single-minded emphasis on the workers' trade union. With the possible exception of some of the Owenites, all the British forerunners of the syndicalists were pluralistic in their conception of socialism. The reformists – the Co-operators and Christian Socialists – did not envisage the abolition of the political State; the revolutionaries – the libertarian socialists and anarchists – while opposing the state idea, did not see the trade union as the only form of organisation in the new society. The trade union was to be only one form among other forms of association – the State of the Commune, the Co-operative Society or the self-governing and spontaneous associations of men for various purposes. The syndicalists, in contrast, were essentially monistic. For them, the trade unions were the only form of organisation which the workers would need under socialism. All social as well as economic activity began and ended in the trade unions. Even where a territorial form of organisation was envisaged as playing its part alongside the functional form of organisation by industry, the unions, and the unions alone, were to be its constituent parts. In this respect, classical syndicalism may be regarded as a narrowing down of hitherto closely-allied ideas, a concentration of them in the one form of organisation which was most clearly related to the intimate and daily experience of the workers. From this concentration syndicalism gathered in strength and gained in clarity – at what, its critics claimed, was the sacrifice of comprehensiveness and other legitimate interests.

This single-minded emphasis on the trade union was the source of much of the distinctive ethos of the movement. The trade union was, at this time, a purely working class form of organisation. In contrast to the so-called workers' political parties or even revolutionary bodies as the *Freedom* group, there was no place in it for anybody who was not a worker. Professional middle class intellectuals who frequently provided both the leadership and the ideas of the socialist political movement, were therefore at a discount. As a consequence the syndicalist movement was, and saw itself as, a purely working class form of socialism – or, as a *Freedom* editorial put it, 'A Working-Class Conception of Socialism'.[5] In retrospect, therefore, syndicalism appears as the great heroic movement of the proletariat, the first movement which took seriously Marx's injunction that the emancipation of the working class must be the task of labour unaided by middle class intellectuals or by politicians and aimed to establish a genuinely working class socialism and culture, free of all bourgeois taints. For the syndicalists, the workers were to be everything, the rest, nothing. The world was to be a world of labour and a world for labour.

Industrial Unionism

Continental syndicalism came to be known as the revision of Marxism 'to the left' in contrast to Bernstein's 'revision to the right'. In these terms, Fabian-Labourism represents the British version of revision to the right. British revision to the left, which marks the beginning of modern syndicalism as a distinct movement in this country, may be dated from the split in the SDF which took place in 1903, and which led to the formation of the Socialist Labour Party. Almost from the outset this party, centred chiefly in Scotland and the North, advocated the cause of industrial unionism and it must be given the credit for introducing this concept in any clear form into this country. Early in its history the party came under the influence of the American Marxist Daniel De Leon, and when the latter joined the Industrial Workers of World, founded at Chicago in 1905, with a programme of militant industrial unionism and workers' control, the SLP became the chief channel of communication between American 'syndicalism' and the British workers. The policy of the SLP is best summed up in its statement: "Having overthrown the class State, the industrial unions will furnish the administrative machinery for directing industry in the Socialist Commonwealth".[6]

In 1905 James Connolly, leader of the Irish Socialist Republican Party, established contact with the SLP on the Clyde and it is in his writings that we find the clearest and most vigorous expression of the ideas dominant during the early phase of the movement. In *Socialism Made Easy* (1908), he argued that the function of industrial unionism was "to build up an industrial republic inside the shell of the political state, in order that when the industrial republic is fully organised, it may crack the shell of the political state and step into its place in the scheme of the universe".[7] Opposing State Socialism as bureaucratic and inimical to individual freedom, he stated that in the form of society he envisaged: "the administration of affairs will be in the hands of the representatives of the various industries of the nation ... The workers in the shops and factories will organise themselves into unions, each union comprising all the workers at a given industry ... [each] union will democratically control the workshop life of its own industry, electing all foreman, etc., and regulating the routine of labour in that industry in subordination to the needs of society in general, to the needs of its allied trades, and to the departments of industry to which it belongs ... Representatives from these various departments of industry will meet and form the industrial administration or national government of the country."[8]

In this industrial republic, the political State would have no place: state, territories and provinces would exist only as geographical expressions. Such a conception of socialism, concluded Connolly, determined the strategy that the working class must pursue. Having realised that "the workshop is the cockpit of civilisation", the workers would recognise that "the fight for the conquest of the political state is not the battle, it is only the echo of the battle. The real battle is the battle being fought out every day for the power to control industry ..."[9]

Syndicalism and the Anarchists

The development of a movement which placed primary emphasis not on political action but on direct action in the industrial field naturally attracted the pure anarchists. In 1903 Samuel Mainwaring had already founded a paper *The General Strike* which, for its short life, became the industrial supplement to *Freedom*, and in 1907 Guy Aldred and Charles Mowbray had formed The Industrial Union of Direct Actionists.[10] Inspired by the libertarian ideas of Bakunin and Kropotkin, its manifesto, addressed "to the Wage Slaves of the World", urged a decentralised pattern of organisation in which each local group of workers would "exercise perfect local autonomy".

Aldred's group, however, was numerically small and soon disappeared. Thus anarchism in Britain provided no Pelloutier to lead the anarchists into the unions and give a libertarian direction to the trade union movement.[11] Dwarfed in size in comparison with the anarchist movement in France, the British anarchist movement at this time was dominated by the ideas of Kropotkin and Malatesta, the leading exponents of anarchist-communism, who had found refuge in this country. Their experience in the First International had convinced them that the trade unions could not be relied upon exclusively. Like all anarchists, Kropotkin accepted the idea of workers' control but he did not stress the need for building up workers' organisations so that they could both fight more effectively in the daily struggle against capitalism and also prepare themselves to become the administrative units of the future society. He took the view, as did most anarchists of that period, that the social revolution would come as a consequence of a general uprising of the whole mass of the people, in the course of which spontaneous associations would be thrown up to carry out the essential work of reconstructing and reorganising society. The single-minded emphasis of the syndicalists on the trade unions, and their assumption that only the activities of the producers really mattered, seemed to him altogether too narrow a doctrine. Thus, when the younger French anarchists were flocking to join the new movement, he pointed out to them that syndicalism was only the partial expression of anarchism as he conceived it.[12]

The Need for Organisation

As against this view, the attitude of the 'pure' syndicalists to anarchism was best expressed by Van Eeden: "Anarchism neglected the immense importance of organisation, and supposed the workers to be capable without leadership, without discipline, of achieving the tremendous task of creating a well-organised commonwealth. This was indeed Utopia in its worse sense. It jumped long periods of slow and difficult education. It did not teach the workers the terrible strength of their opponents, the exploiters. It did not realise how the intricate structure of modern society demanded great organising capacities, scientific knowledge, economical insight, first-rate leadership, and strict discipline, in order to replace the old order by a new and better one. So anarchism was soon paralysed and left behind in the struggle. It could strike, but not conquer. It proved to be destructive, not constructive. It withered for want of successful deeds."[13]

The new ferment in the industrial world did, however, result in the anarchists turning their attention once again to the trade unions. John Turner of the shopworkers, for example, started, early in 1907, *The Voice of Labour* which devoted itself to trade union problems and Kropotkin himself came round to the view that the anarchists might usefully permeate the unions.[14] It was now Malatesta's turn to advise caution. The unions, he argued, contained valuable sources of strength but also elements of reaction; anarchists, therefore, should not identify themselves too closely with syndicalism.[15]

Despite their ambivalent attitude during this period, the anarchists had, in the words of the historian of British syndicalism, "provided a steady stream of propaganda, information and discussion upon the developments of French syndicalism and, to a lesser degree, of American syndicalism. Their long, involved and desultory debate on syndicalism had not resulted any marked coalescence of the two movements, but it had assured that a considerable group of Englishmen were conscious of the progress of syndicalist ideas".[16]

The Industrial Syndicalist Education League

In 1910, with the return to England of Tom Mann, the British syndicalist movement emerged from the half-light into the full glare of day. From his eight years in Australia and New Zealand, Mann had acquired a knowledge of industrial unionism and a profound sense of disillusionment with regard to attempts to establish industrial peace. Shortly after his return, accompanied by Guy Bowman, a socialist journalist, he visited France and contacted the Confédération Général du Travail. Filled with enthusiasm, they started, when they came back, the publication of *The Industrial Syndicalist*[17] and later in the same year founded The Industrial Syndicalist Education League. The conscious adoption of the name 'syndicalist' heralded the development of a British form of syndicalism which, although it borrowed widely from the French and American movements, was to have a distinctive character of its own. Revolutionary as Mann was, he remained essentially of a practical turn of mind and the main activities of the new body, which quickly attracted to itself many of the 'syndicalists' of the other groups, were confined to educational propaganda on the subject of industrial unionism. Attempts were made by Mann and his associates to persuade the older unions to federate or to amalgamate on industrial lines and to give a revolutionary turn to the industrial unrest which, for a wide variety of reasons, swept the country in the year 1911. In the main these activities belong to social and trade union history, but out of the welter of these years emerged, in 1912, what has now come to be regarded as the classic statement of British syndicalism: *The Miners' Next Step*.[18]

The Miners' Next Step

This pamphlet was not, however, intended as a definitive statement of syndicalist thought. Its subtitle, *A suggested scheme for the reorganisation of the Federation*, and its foreword clearly indicated that it was to be taken as no more than an agenda for future discussions among the South Wales Miners. From our point of view, what is of chief interest about its plans for the immediate reorganisation of the Miners' Federation is its insistence on the need for centralisation combined with measures designed to retain power in the hands of the rank and file. On the question of political action, it takes up the position of the SLP: "complete independence of, and hostility to, all capitalist parties", while the long term objective of the authors is summed up in the words: Industrial Democracy. "The men who work in the mine", they argue, "are surely as competent to elect these [paid officials] as shareholders who may never have seen a colliery. To have a vote in deciding who shall be your fireman, manager, inspector, etc., is to have a vote in determining the conditions which shall rule your working life ... To vote for a man to represent you in Parliament, to make rules for, and assist in appointing officials to rule you, is a different proposition altogether!" Nationalisation of the mines, they continue, is no step towards industrial democracy; it "simply makes a National Trust, with all the force of Government behind it, whose one concern will be to see that the industry is run in such a way as to pay the interest on the bonds, with which the Coal-owners are paid out, and to extract as much more profit as possible, in order to relieve the taxation of other landlords and capitalists."

The pamphlet concludes with a vision of the future society: "Every industry thoroughly organised, in the first place, to fight, to gain control of, and then to administer, that industry. The co-ordination of all industries on a Central Production Board, who, with a statistical department to ascertain the needs of the people, will issue demands to the different departments of industry, leaving to the men themselves to determine under what conditions, and how, the work should be done. This would mean real democracy in real life making for real manhood and womanhood. Any other form of democracy is a snare and a delusion."

It would be a mistake, however, to regard the ideas contained in this famous pamphlet as completely representative of the views of the British syndicalists of this period. Scattered among the various articles and speeches on the subject of reorganising trade unionism are to be found numerous references to the future society which amplify and in some respects contradict the views of the South

Wales miners' unofficial committee, and there exist several books and pamphlets which are directly concerned with theoretical problems. British syndicalism never found its Sorel. In this it was both fortunate and unfortunate. Fortunate in that it escaped that form of misrepresentation which the French movement suffered when intellectuals like Sorel, Berth and Lagardelle were accepted by the outside world as theorists of the new socialism; unfortunate in that it was unable to clarify some of its basic concepts or to answer effectively the criticisms of opponents, both socialist and anti-socialist, when they ignorantly and often perversely misread its intentions. The anti-intellectual tendencies of the French movement have been grossly exaggerated even by historians. In England, there is little or no trace of anti-intellectualism, although there is evidence of open hostility towards middle class theorists – a very different thing.

The Syndicalist Commonwealth

The men who paid most attention to the theoretical aspects of syndicalism and the future society were Tom Mann, Guy Bowman and Gaylord Wilshire. Mann in 1913 defined syndicalism in the following terms: "A condition of society where industry will be controlled by those engaged therein, on the basis of free societies; these co-operate for the production of all requirements of life in the most efficient manner, and the distribution of the same with the truest equity; a society in which Parliament and Governments will have disappeared, having served their purpose with the capitalist system".[19]

From Single Tax to Syndicalism contains Mann's developed views on syndicalist organisation and its chief interest, in this respect, lies in the place he assigns to the Trades Councils – the British equivalent to the French Bourses du Travail. In Mann's view, the Trades Councils were an essential element in syndicalist organisation, their function being to ascertain the needs of people in their respective districts and to arrange distribution.

Bowman, too, emphasised the role of the Trades Councils. While differing from the French syndicalists in proposing *amalgamation* of existing trade unions to form industrial unions, in place of the French national federations which did not necessarily involve the establishment of unions along the lines of industries, his main organisational proposals were modelled closely on those of the French CGT as expounded by Pataud and Pouget in their book, *Syndicalism and the Co-operative Commonwealth*.[20] The Industrial Unions were to form a National Federation of Industrial Unions and the Trades Councils a National Federation of Trades Councils; then both of these federations were to be confederated in a General Confederation of Labour, which would thus include all producers and distributors. Since both producers and distributors were also consumers, there would be no need for special arrangements to represent the consumers as such. Production would be the task of the Industrial Unions, and the Trades Councils would provide the machinery for local distribution and administration. The Trades Councils, which since their exclusion from the TUC in 1895 had become mere adjuncts of political advancement, would, according to Bowman, have to "stand against the municipal council, destroy it, and establish themselves in its place".[21]

Mann and Bowman were successful in pressing their views on the delegates to the syndicalist conferences held in Manchester and in London, November 1912. These conferences were designed mainly to give a more definitive statement of the programme and aims of the British syndicalist movement, and resolutions embodying Bowman's proposals were adopted almost unanimously.[22]

Syndicalism and Ownership

Gaylord Wilshire's main contribution to syndicalist thought was to emphasise its communistic basis and to rebut the charges brought against the syndicalists that ownership of industries by the workers employed in them would be as anti-social as ownership by capitalist syndicates. It is possible that certain syndicalists imagined that the adoption of the slogans 'The mine for the miners', 'The railway for the railwaymen', and so on, meant that the workers of a particular industry would jointly become the 'owners' of their industry and, as such, would share any 'profits' that were made.

The simplest way of grasping the syndicalist idea is to think of it as producers' co-operation organised under the auspices of industrial unions and enlarged to national dimensions. However, without qualification, this conception can be misleading. There is no evidence that syndicalists thought in terms of 'co-ownership' and 'profit-sharing' and, indeed, these notions were explicitly repudiated on several occasions.[23] The main tendency of syndicalist thought, it may be said, was to undermine the concept of ownership as it is commonly understood. There is an implicit recognition of the fact that ownership as such is unimportant: what matters is control – who shall control industry and in whose interests that control be exercised. The syndicalists stood for control of industry by the workers in the interests of the workers. Although they often repeated the age-old demand that the workers had the right to the whole produce of their labour, they did not, in the main, interpret this to mean that each group of workers should receive the full fruits of its labours, or that each individual should be so rewarded. Behind the slogan was little more than the demand that labour *as a whole* should enjoy what it had produced; in other words, that capitalist profit-makers, rentiers and interest receivers should be eliminated.

Bowman in this respect took up the position of the pure communist. "In the society we sydicalists wish to bring about", he said, "there shall be no *value* whatever attached to any commodity, so that every individual will be able to partake of all commodities in the full measure of his needs". Wilshire, more cautiously, thought that remuneration might be determined either by deeds or by needs "as may hereafter be decided". What would certainly *not* be the basis of remuneration was the importance of an individual's product to the community. That "would be merely changing the present system, with a myriad of exploiting workers".[24] Syndicalism, he insisted, meant that the control of the technical processes now exercised by the capitalists would pass to groups of organised workers of the various industries. The product, however, which was now the property of the capitalists would become, under syndicalism, the property of the community.

Syndicalist Controversies

Despite the tendency towards anarchism and communism displayed by the later syndicalists, there were concealed differences of attitude which made relations between the anarchists and the syndicalists somewhat less than harmonious. The anarchists 'captured' *The Syndicalist* in December 1913, and joined the small group of British 'Wobblies' in condemning moderates like Mann, Tillett, Lansbury and Larkin who were content to advocate amalgamation as a step towards industrial unionism. This policy, they argued, savoured of opportunism. Underlying this difference as regards *means* was, however, a difference, so far as the anarchists were concerned, as regards *ends*. Despite the adoption, largely under Bowman's guidance, of what were essentially French ideas of organisation, it was not altogether clear how they fitted in with the organisation of *national* industrial unions. Pataud and Pouget's book was written at a time when most of the French trade unions or syndicats were still local bodies and soon after the CGT had received a new lease of life from its federation in 1902 with the Bourses du Travail. This fact, as well as their origin, explains Pataud and Pouget's emphasis on decentralisation. At the time when the main outlines of the French structure were being adopted by British syndicalists, the CGT itself was becoming much more reticent about the future society. Their reticence, which was associated with a greater emphasis on revolutionary direct action, was partly the result of a change in industrial organisation in France. There was a marked trend towards national organisation of trade unions and the Bourses declined in importance within the French movement. In these circumstances, it could be that their original theory was fast becoming obsolete. "They have not", said Cole, "thought out a new system of organisation capable of supplanting capitalism in such a way as to accept as its basis national trade unionism".[25]

Anarchist Criticisms

British trade unionism had from the start of the syndicalist movement been predominantly national in character; hence its insistence on *national* industrial unions. Although the federal principle found its place within Bowman's proposed structure – in linking up the unions and the trade councils and then both in the General Confederation of Labour – it found no place *inside* the industrial unions to which were assigned the tasks of production. The anarchists, who were *par excellence* the exponents of the principles of federalism and local autonomy, suspected that the industrial unions might become unwieldy, bureaucratic and, in the end, tyrannical organisations. Moreover, attempts to reconcile interests in the national level in a central confederative council involved obvious dangers. Although the functions of the central body were to be statistical and informative only, it might easily develop into what would be, on an industrial instead of a territorial basis, a state in all but name. The centralist tendencies seem evident in sections of *The Miners' Next Step* seemed to confirm anarchist suspicions, especially as one of its authors had previously advocated a plebiscitary form of trade union leadership.[26] The attitude of the anarchist syndicalists was expressed thus: "Syndicalists stand for the individual, and are therefore as much opposed to the Industrial State as to the Political State. Actually, we object to an Industrial State even more strenuously than we do to a Political State; for under the second there are at least some people who are free, but under the first there would not be one man or woman left free".[27] Following this line of thought, the anarchists laid primary emphasis on "the autonomous workshops controlled through a shop committee" rather than on industrial unions.

A further aspect of this conflict between anarchists and syndicalists becomes clear when it is appreciated that the syndicalists accepted implicitly the large scale organisation of industry. In this their Marxist orientation is evident. They wished to adapt syndicalist theories to industrial organisation rather than industrial organisation to syndicalist theories, and indeed the whole tenor of their propaganda was that the workers must reorganise so that they could achieve the powerful unity which, it was alleged, the capitalists were achieving. Among the anarchists, however, there was a latent and, in the case of Kropotkin, an open hostility towards large scale industry.[28] They recognised that freedom could not easily be achieved in modern industrialised society with its marked emphasis on the interdependence of all groups. They felt that the more complex became society, the larger the scale of organisation, the narrower became the chances of the individual finding the freedom with which to develop himself as he saw fit.

The Amalgamation Movement

The conflicts within the syndicalist movement as the First World War approached weakened the effectiveness of its propaganda. By the end of 1913 the ISEL had shifted its base to the Industrial Democracy League which was active in South Wales and which concentrated on the reform of trade union structure rather than on revolutionary action. The IWW, critical of this passive role, formed its own British Administration and published a short-lived paper, *The Industrial Worker*, 1913-14. British syndicalists, however, could not be persuaded of the necessity of building up new industrial unions from scratch on the IWW model. During the war attempts were made to place the British Administration on a firmer basis but it never succeeded in becoming an influential force. As far as the anarchists were concerned, the outbreak of war split them into two sections, an important minority led by Kropotkin urging that a victory of the Central Powers must be avoided at all costs. *The Voice of Labour* continued publication until 1916 but exerted little influence on syndicalist thought and action. With its demise the anarchist conception of syndicalism disappeared for a time to re-emerge later in the form of anarcho-syndicalism. The main body of syndicalists continued to press the idea of amalgamation and to this end set up the Amalgamated Committees' Federation which had as its object: "To prepare the workers for their economic emancipation by their taking possession of the means of production and distribution through an economic organisation outside the control of any parliamentary party or religious sect".

The Workers' Committee Movement

Meanwhile an independent movement, largely composed of new men and influenced by the SLP, had sprung up on Clydeside and spread rapidly to Sheffield and other industrial centres. The Clyde

Workers' committee was composed of people who accepted the full revolutionary implications of industrial unionism and their connection with the mainstream of syndicalism cannot be doubted. The Workers' Committees were a rank and file movement drawing support from those who were critical of the official trade union leadership which had given its support to the war effort. After a conference of these committees a national organisation was set up and in 1917 it joined forces with the amalgamation movement. The fusion of forces was not, however, altogether satisfactory and at the last Rank and File Conference held in October 1917, there was serious disagreement between those who wished to form an industrial union and those who wished to concentrate their energies on the workers' committee movement. J.T. Murphy, the chief spokesman of the latter group, evolved a plan for a rank and file organisation to be built upon industrial lines.[29] The workshops were to be the basic units of the new organisation, with shop stewards represented on Works Committees and, indirectly, through them, on National Industrial Committees. From these national committees a National Administrative Council would be formed as a counterpart of the TUC. The plan closely resembled the existing trade union structure except that it was put on an industrial and not on a craft and territorial basis. Murphy contended that the proposed organisation was not an alternative to the existing structure and that the committees were not intended to usurp the functions of the executives of the trade unions. The exact relationship between the two movements was not, however, clearly defined and the official leaders naturally suspected the worst.

Encroaching control

The chief interest of the Workers' Committee Movement from our point of view, however, lies in its production of the policy of 'encroaching control' through the application of the 'collective contract'. Two of the members associated with the movement – W. Gallacher of the Clyde Workers' Committee and John Paton of the ASE – published in 1917 a memorandum entitled *Towards Industrial Democracy*. The Works Committees, it was suggested, once they had gained experience and authority, should "undertake in one large contract, or in two or three contracts at the most, the entire business of production throughout the establishment". In this way, the functions of management would gradually pass to the committees. The workers, it was argued, already ultimately pay all the expenses of management without enjoying any of its privileges. By instituting democratic workshops, the number of functionaries could be greatly reduced and many of the species in "the army of managers, foremen, bullies, speeders-up and spies who throng our industry today" entirely eliminated. Once the committees had obtained a foothold in management they could use their position, by raising the terms of the contract so as to get the full exchange value of their products, to deliver the knock-out blow to capitalism.

The collective contract was thus conceived mainly, as a tactical device to obtain control of industry on syndicalist lines. But it does also illustrate the real significance and the strong appeal of syndicalism. The syndicalists said, in effect, that the revolution must begin in the workshop. Their message to the workers was much the same as Goethe's to the emigrant in search of liberty: "Here, or nowhere, is your America!" Here, in the workshop, in the factory and in the mine, they said, we must accomplish the revolution or it will be accomplished nowhere. So long as we are a subject class industrially, so long will we remain a subject class politically. The real revolution must be made not in Parliament or at the barricades but in the places where we earn our daily bread. The organisations that we build up to carry on the daily struggle must be the foundations of the new order and we must be its architects. The law and morality that we have evolved in our long struggle with capitalism must be the law and morality of the future workers' commonwealth. All other proposals are but snares and delusions.

Disintegration of the Syndicalist Movement

The differences evident at the Fifth Rank and File Conference of the amalgamation movement were, however, the prelude to the disintegration of syndicalism. Already political agitation was undermining the non-political character of the movement with its single-minded emphasis on economic action and organisation. The March Revolution in Russia had already occurred and the subsequent October Revolution gave an added impetus to the political tendencies. In the excitement occasioned by the events in Russia, many syndicalists forgot the text they had preached and hitherto acted upon: that no new system can supersede another until it has become fully matured within the womb of the old. Convinced that a revolution was nearer than they had dared to hope, they abandoned their faith in purely industrial action and began to realign themselves with those groups and parties which aimed at a revolutionary capture of political power. Many of them, especially those connected with the SLP, and including Tom Mann, joined the Communist Party of Great Britain after its foundation in August 1920. Once within the party their anti- parliamentarianism rapidly dissolved before the criticisms of Lenin.

Other elements found temporary refuge within the Guild Socialist movement which had taken up and transmuted many of the older movement's ideas. The anarchist version of syndicalism still claimed a few supporters who clung all the more determinedly to their faith when they saw the way the revolution was developing in Russia. In 1922 at a conference in Berlin the anarchist wing refused to enter the Red Trade Union International (The Profintern) and put forward a theory of anarcho-syndicalism. The development of this movement belongs more to foreign – especially Spanish – than to British history, but it is significant to note that it was the anarchists with their long tradition of hostility towards political action who, despite their differences with the movement, remained true to the militant aspirations of syndicalism. In this country pure syndicalism has been bequeathed as a legacy to the anarchists who, since the Spanish Civil War, have placed increasing emphasis on its ideas.

"Consolidation and Control"

For the main body of syndicalist thought a suitable obituary notice is to be found in the publication in 1921 of a pamphlet by the National Workers' Committee Movement entitled *Consolidation and Control*. The pamphlet emphasised much of what had already been stated in Murphy's earlier pamphlet; the class consciousness so characteristic of syndicalism was no less evident; and the elimination of the capitalists from industry was pronounced as the goal. But it went on to subject the notion of workers' control to critical scrutiny. It noted its ambiguity now that it had been taken up by many elements in Labour Party and by the Guild Socialists. It criticised the then current proposals for State ownership combined with joint State-Union management. It decried the uncritical acceptance of the notion that the State was the representative of the community. The State, it insisted, was and always had been an engine of the ruling class and could not therefore represent both contending classes in society.

So far nothing had been subtracted from and little added to the syndicalist case. But then came the sting in the tail. "The problem that is facing the working class", it said "is the problem of power ... If the workers' organisations are victorious in the struggle, then they will become the foundations of the new working class State. The unions will share with the State the control and management of the large-scale industries, and from this a system of workers' control will be developed. The exact amount of industrial control that the average worker will get following a working class victory will depend upon the circumstances. We do not believe that it is possible to jump from a system, where the mass of workers who have lived most of their lives under the control of the functionaries of capitalism will suddenly be able to select those who are competent to carry on the management of industry from the workshop upwards. Such ability will only come as the result of education and opportunity, but it is the end we are striving for. There may be a period short or long according to the circumstances when control and management will be from above. That is to say, when those who direct industry shall be appointed not by the workers in industry, but by the workers' state, the voice of the unions in the matter being comparatively slight."

Syndicalism and the Communists

Despite the insistence that workers' control was still the ultimate aim, it is clear that the movement was to be subordinated to the political party which aimed at a revolutionary overthrow of the capitalist State and the establishment of the dictatorship of the proletariat. The idea of encroaching control by means of the collective contract which had expressed most clearly the syndicalist contention that the revolution must begin in the workshop if it was to begin at all, was rudely dismissed. Its remaining author[30] now regarded it as embarrassing evidence of his 'infantile leftism'. The workshop organisation should be pre-eminently one designed for fighting and should not saddle itself with responsibilities. Its function was to break up workshop discipline and make the system as unworkable as possible. The most damning word in the new vocabulary was hurled at it: it was 'utopian'. Finally, in a conclusion, it might be admitted that "*a limited amount* of self-government in the workshops will be one of the things achieved by the workers' state *in the course of time.*[31] That it can be achieved under capitalism is simply a delusion of those who imagine that the control of industry can be gradually wrested from the employers without their power being first broken."

. The syndicalists who took path and joined the Communist Party did not, I think, feel that they were betraying their past. On the contrary, they probably felt that they were making an advance towards reality when they put the conquest of political power first. Many of them may indeed have thought that a dictatorship of the proletariat would really lead to workers' control in the full-blooded sense and to the establishment of the industrial commonwealth in which the trade unions would come into their own. If so, they were either cruelly deluded or bitterly disillusioned by subsequent events.

So ended the syndicalist movement. I have dealt with it at some length because so far no objective account of it has been published – although a full-scale history of the movement, written, be it noted, by an American not a British student, lies in the inaccessible archives of Oxford's Bodleian Library. In most, if not all, available histories of the British working class movement the contribution of the British syndicalists to the popularising of the notion of workers' control in this period has been seriously underestimated. The British syndicalists produced no great library of theoretical works and the development of the movement and its ideas must be traced in dusty files scattered in many libraries. But what they did write and, more important, what they uttered by the spoken word – Tom Mann was perhaps the last of the line of working class orators in this country – reached a not inconsiderable section of rank and file industrial workers. Moreover, the movement remains of more than historical interest. The controversies within it over the organisation of the future society and the strategy to be pursued to achieve workers' control are still very much alive – and contain lessons which still have to be learned if industrial freedom is ever to be won.

Guild Socialism

Perhaps the principal explanation of why the British syndicalist movement has been neglected by historians is that it was overshadowed by the Guild Socialist movement which flourished in this country between 1912 and 1924. It has now become customary to regard Guild Socialism as the adaptation of syndicalist theories to British conditions. The syndicalists themselves viewed the matter somewhat differently: "Middle-class of the middle-class, with all the shortcomings (we almost said 'stupidities') of the middle-class writ large across it", declared one syndicalist writer. "'Guild Socialism' stands forth as the latest lucubration of the middle-class mind. It is a 'cool steal' of the leading ideas of Syndicalism and a deliberate perversion of them ... We do protest against the 'State' idea ... in Guild Socialism. Middle-class people, even when they become socialists, cannot get rid of the idea that the working class is their 'inferior'; that the workers need to be 'educated', drilled, disciplined, and generally nursed for a long time before they will be able to walk by themselves. The very reverse is actually the truth".[32]

There is a good deal of truth in both these points of view, so far as they go, but both obscure certain aspects of the Guild Socialist movement which derived little or no inspiration from Syndicalism and both ignore the deep roots that the new movement had in the English radical and socialist tradition. It would perhaps be more true to say that Guild Socialism was the amalgam of very different and even diverse elements of which syndicalism was the most obvious if also the most important.

The Restoration of the Guild System

In its earliest manifestations the new movement had nothing whatever to do with either French syndicalism or American industrial unionism. As the title of the book which can be said to mark the formal beginning of the movement makes clear, it was at this nebulous stage a backward rather than a forward-looking movement. This book, *The Restoration of the Gild System* by A.J. Penty was published in 1906, but it had been 'on the stocks' since the turn of the century and its contents had been known to a small circle of Penty's friends who shared his dislike of current Fabianism. Penty's book, the preface to which acknowledged the influence of Ruskin and Carpenter, was an attempt to give a practical direction to the artistic tradition in British socialism. In it can be found some of the leading ideas of later guildsmen together with many that remained largely his own. For Penty the great evil of modern society was not the private ownership of capital or the competition that went with it but commercialism and the control of industry by the financier in place of the master craftsman. Commercialism, he argued, led to the debasement of moral and aesthetic values and destroyed the craftsman's pride and joy in his work. Collectivism or State Socialism ignored these spiritual values and was, in effect, merely 'State Commercialism'. "The mere transference of the control of industry from the hands of the capitalists into those of the State can make no essential difference to the nature of the industry affected". Collectivism rested on the fallacy that Government should be conducted solely in the interests of man in his capacity as consumer: a true system would aim at a just balance between consumer and producer. The real reformer, concluded Penty, must therefore boldly set his face against the further evolution of society in the direction in which it was moving. Social salvation could only come with the re-introduction of the medieval gild system of organisation under which producers, working in their small and separate workshops, would be subject to the regulation of their appropriate gild.

The Rise of Guild Socialism

The publication of Penty's book was planned as the first move in the formation of a Gilds Restoration League, a statement of whose objects included: "The principle of the Gild System is true for all time. It is the principle that individual craftsmen should in all matters relating to his craft be subject to the control of the craft to which he belongs ... The foundations of a restored Gild System have already been laid in the Trade Union and the Arts and Crafts Movements. These two represent respectively an economic and an artistic revolt, the former seeking to emancipate the worker and the latter seeking to emancipate the craft, from the spirit of commercialism".[33]

The ideas behind the abortive League were carried into the citadel of collectivism itself with the formation in 1907, by A.R. Orage and Holbrook Jackson, of the Fabian Arts Group; but the group failed to flourish and speedily came to an end.

The New Age

In the same year, however, Orage and Jackson took over the editorship of *The New Age*, a weekly review which was to play an important part in the development of Guild Socialist thought. The new editors displayed a catholic taste, the review became the forum for a large number of gifted and independently-minded writers of all political complexions, and it rapidly won for itself the reputation of being the most stimulating product in contemporary journalism. Articles on the arts and crafts movement received due place in its columns and Penty, for a time, continued his assaults on collectivism, large-scale organisation and modern industrialism. Of greater immediate influence, however, were the writings of Belloc and Chesterton who developed in its pages and elsewhere their distributivist theories and who sounded the alarm against the approach of the Servile State. Their distributivist ideals left no impression on guild theories but their anti-collectivism added point and vigour to Penty's attack. In his editorial Notes of the Week, Orage, with skill and subtlety, translated their hostility towards state action into socialist language. All the much vaunted reforms of the Liberals, which were supported by the Labour Party and the Fabians, were serving, he argued, only to make capitalism more endurable by rendering the working classes slightly more comfortable. Such provisions as the new conciliation and arbitration boards not only assumed an equality between the parties which did not exist – while at the same time restricting the freedom of trade union action – but they were based on the "insufferable hypothesis" that "the status of the wage-slave" was to be a permanent feature of society. The Webbites – "particularly efficient worryguts of the poor" – and Fabians generally might produce grand schemes for the amelioration of the working classes but they should not forget, he said, that there was "a group of socialists who have as yet found no convenient label, but who will have no curtailment of liberty, no coercion of the individual, although it come with material benefit".[34]

The columns of *The New Age* in the years 1908-12 reflect another factor which was strongly to shape Guild doctrines – the steadily mounting disillusionment of the more militant socialists with Labour politics. Cecil Chesterton, for example, contributed a series of articles on 'How the Rich Rule Us' from which Orage drew the conclusion that "politics, like capital, is an exclusive possession of the governing classes". The moral pointed was that Trade Unions should stick to their own field, concentrate on economics and leave politics to take care of itself – a foreshadowing of what was to become almost an axiom of Guild Socialist thinking that economic power precedes and dominates political power.

As befitted a journal of the avant-garde, *The New Age* was one of the first widely-read journals to take note of the new ideas of syndicalism that were developing rapidly in France. With a characteristic perversity, however, it refused to believe that syndicalism had taken roots in England. Nevertheless, it was quick to interpret the current 'industrial unrest' in the light of the central idea of syndicalism – workers' control. Failing socialisation, it suggested, there should be established a 'co-partnery' in which the unions as corporate bodies and gilds should be associated in joint responsibility with the owners of capital. The gild system, it went on to claim, was "a genuine Saxon invention, as native to our genius as our language. The true line of development of our trade unions is, therefore, most certainly in the direction of the restoration of the essential features of the gild system – the responsibility for skilled work, the discipline of its members, the disposition of its collective forces and the joint control with their clients (employers in this instance) of the whole range of industry".[35]

National Guilds

With the publication on 25th April 1912 of an article entitled 'Emancipation and the Wage System', the guild movement entered a new phase in which the arts and crafts side and the Medievalism of Penty were to drop into the background and Marxian economics and industrial 'politics' were to come to the fore. (The use of the less archaic form of spelling 'guild' marked the new phase of the movement). The article, the first of a series, was the work of S.G. Hobson, a veteran socialist and journalist. In 1914 the articles were republished in book form under the title *National Guilds: an inquiry into the wage system and the way out*. They mark the first definite formulation of the new school of socialist thought and the book soon became almost the standard text of the movement.

The fundamental fact of modern social and industrial organisation, argued Hobson, is the existence of the wage system by which the capitalist produces wares and is enabled to sell them at a profit. Under this system labour is assumed to be purely and simply a commodity to be bought and sold like any other commodity. In return for the sale of his labour power, the worker receives wages, i.e. the price of labour established in the market by the operation of the laws of supply and demand. These laws result in wages approximating to the cost of subsistence necessary to maintain and to reproduce labour power. When the worker sells his labour power to an employer, the labour becomes the property of the buyer, the producer loses all control over the products he makes, and he admits the right of the employer to dictate the conditions of his employment. This right allows the buyer to terminate employment at will, with the result that the seller has no security. The receipt of wages is thus the mark of a subject class. So long as the wage system remains, the status of the recipients of wages will be an inferior one and, in essentials, no different from that of the chattel slave. This system, continued Hobson, is based on two false assumptions, namely, that labour, having sold, has no kind of economic or social claim to the products of labour. There could be no emancipation of labour until these two assumptions were exposed and the wage system destroyed.

A Brotherhood of Producers

Turning to his constructive proposals, Hobson rejected Orage's idea of a 'co-partnery' between the employers and the unions. By a series of steps – making themselves black-leg proof, striking not for higher wages but for superior status, and amalgamating and federating on an industrial basis – the trade unions, argued Hobson, could abolish the wage system completely and effect a total social reconstruction. Under the new system that could succeed the wage system, producers would be recognised and paid as human beings, receiving payment in and out of employment, in sickness and in health; would share co-operatively in the organisation of production; and together would exercise a claim on the product of their work. Such a system could best be organised under modern industrial conditions if producers were banded together in National Guilds. A National Guild would be "a self-governing brotherhood of producers", possessing a monopoly of labour in its particular industry. It would embrace all grades of workers, manual, technical and managerial, i.e. 'the salariat' as well as the proletariat. Assuming complete responsibility for the material welfare of its members, it would become a fellowship as well as an economic organisation.

About fourteen National Guilds were envisaged, each of which would receive from the State a charter giving it responsibility for the management of its particular industry. Ownership would be formally vested in the State but all property would be held 'in trust' by the Guilds. In return for their charters, the Guilds would pay to the State "a substitute for economic rent". The Guilds would not act independently of each other but would all be represented on a Guilds Congress, the successor of the TUC. This Congress would sit in permanent session and would become "the directorate of industry". Any negotiations with the State would be conducted through the officers of the Congress. In the new society, the State would take on its true role as representative of the whole community: State control of the Guilds would operate in a manner similar to the control exercised by shareholders at present; and the political system, purified of all economic responsibility, could henceforth concern itself with 'the national soul'.

The Greater Unionism

The publication of the National Guilds articles aroused considerable discussion in intellectual and socialist circles and the movement began to win adherents, particularly among the younger socialists. The most important of these was G.D.H. Cole in whose hands guild theories were to be considerably elaborated and in some important respects transformed. His position in the Labour movement made him an admirable vehicle for the propagation of guild views. In collaboration with William Mellor of the Fabian Research Department, he began to develop in *The Daily Herald* and other Labour papers the idea of the Greater Unionism, the chief principles of which were: the sinking of craft and sectional interests; organisation on a workshop and industrial basis; the inclusion of brain workers in the ranks of the unions; the achievement of a black-leg-proof and united Labour Movement; and a change in trade union policy in preparation for the future task of administering national industries in conjunction with the State.[36]

In 1915 a new phase of the movement began with the establishment by Cole and his friends of The National Guilds League. Like the Fabian Society, the League did not attempt to become a mass organisation and its membership never exceeded 600, the majority of whom were middle-class professional people with a sprinkling of trade unionists. It soon included in its ranks, however, some of the ablest writers of the day such as Bertrand Russell, R.H. Tawney, H.N. Brailsford, George Lansbury and Norman Angell. The activities of the League, which included after December 1916 the publication of a journal, *The Guildsman*, later *The Guild Socialist*, were inevitably hampered by wartime conditions but, on the other hand, the war also created conditions favourable to the reception of its propaganda by the younger trade union elements and by those active in the Shop Stewards' Movement. Most of the leaflets and pamphlets of the NGL were directed to trade unionists and elaborated the steps whereby Guilds might be formed in particular industries. This translation of Guild ideas into an effective movement did not, however, prevent the guildsmen examining more thoroughly their theoretical concepts and attempting to draw a more detailed picture of the working of the future Guild Commonwealth.

Industrial Democracy and Management

One problem which much pre-occupied the theorists of the movement was the application of democratic principles to management. In *National Guilds* Hobson assumed that workmen could be trusted to elect the best people as managers and that since the basis of choice would be widened, there would be no danger of inefficient management. As the guildsmen came to grips with this subject the question of democratic management was dismissed in a less cavalier fashion. There remained, however, among many a tendency to regard the function of management as one not so difficult as sometimes alleged: "With but a little extra training many of the rank and file could become technicians capable of filling any of the administrative and scientific posts".[37] This optimism was not shared by all. Some thought that democratic election was suitable for the lower grades but that for the higher grades the principle of elevation by one's peers or even appointment from above should be employed. Others considered that every official in the main framework of the Guilds should be chosen, not by general election, but by men best qualified to judge of their ability for the position, provided that every such choice was ratified by the men affected by it. "The Guild would build up in this way a pyramid of officers, each chosen by the grade immediately below that which [the officer] is to occupy".[38] Yet another suggestion was that there should be a panel of managers from which the National Guild Executive would allocate individuals to particular works, again subject to the approval of the workers there. A similar panel of foremen would be selected by the works committees.[39]

It remained for Cole, however, to attempt an analysis of the function of management and on the basis of that analysis to work out a detailed scheme of industrial democracy. A suitable text for discussion was provided by the arch-priest of Fabian Collectivism, Sidney Webb, in his *The Works Manager Today*, 1917. Webb was concerned to argue that management was, or was becoming, a specialist technique: "What we are concerned with here, whether we are considering any grade of managers or superintendents, is the quite distinct profession of organising men – of so arranging and dictating the activities of a band of producers, including both brain and manual workers, and to create amongst them the most effective co-operation of their energies. What the manager has principally to handle, therefore, is not wood or metal but human nature, not machinery but will ... In my opinion, the profession of manager, under whatever designation ... is destined, with the ever-increasing complication of man's enterprises, to develop a steadily increasing technique and a more and more specialised training of its own; and to secure, like the vocation of the engineer, the architect, or the chemist, universal recognition as a specialised brain-working occupation".[40]

The Manipulation of Men

Cole denied that 'the manipulation of men' was a science to be learned and controlled by experts. There was a fundamental difference, he argued, between such professions as medicine and architecture and the 'profession' of manager in that the latter is primarily a disciplinarian, whereas the former are concerned to provide technical advice. The manager resembled more the professional politician or the administrative Civil Servant than either the doctor or architect. It would, therefore, be "as dangerous to endow him with the full status of a governing profession as it is to endow the politician or the bureaucrat with full authority". For this reason, "just as the community ought to demand and maintain democratic control over its political administrators, so Industrial Labour will claim direct democratic control over those who seek to manipulate its industrial conditions".[41]

The distinction between the technician and the manipulator of men provided, in Cole's view, a rough guide in the method of appointment in an industrial democracy. The technical and commercial experts could not be chosen by democratic vote since the electors were not competent to judge the experts' qualifications. It would suffice that they should be the servants of a democratically elected authority such as the national executive committee of a Guild. In cases where managers were also required to be technicians, the possession of definite qualifications of skill and technique would be made a condition of their eligibility for managerial positions. "A ship owner today can only appoint as captain of his ship a man who holds a master's certificate. The seamen of the future Guild will only be able to choose as their captain a man who is similarly equipped".[42] As to the basis of election, Cole argued that the officials must, if freedom is to be a reality in the Guild, be under the control of those they direct.[43]

Cole was hopeful that a democratic regime in industry would have a special appeal to managerial elements. The manager would not have the uncontrolled power to dismiss workers, nor would he be able to ignore public opinion either in the factory or in the Guild. On the other hand, when the rank and file secured not only a direct interest in production but also the means of making their wills effective, it was hoped that the manager would be faced not with apathy or hostility but with a co-operative attitude on the part of all workers. In any case, he would not be in the awkward position of being the nominee of a capitalist employer. "I strongly suspect", concluded Cole, "that the managers in a Guild factory would have no cause to complain of lack of power. If they wanted authority, they would find ample scope for it; but I believe most of them would soon cease to think of their positions mainly in terms of power, and would come to think of them mainly in terms of function. Only under the free conditions of democratic industry would the leader find real scope for leadership, and he would find it in a way that would enable him to concentrate all his faculties on the development of his factory as a communal service, instead of being, as now, constantly thwarted and restrained by considerations of shareholders' profits".[44]

The Guilds and the State

One of the weakest points in the original formulation of National Guilds theory by Hobson was the definition of the relation between the Guilds and the State. The State was to be shorn of its economic and financial responsibilities while, at the same, retaining in the interests of the community the ultimate right to control policy. The conclusion drawn by many critics was that in matters of dispute either the State would coerce the Guilds, which would bring us back to the Collectivist position, or the Guilds would over-rule the State and we should be very near to syndicalism. The answer that this would be avoided because both State and Guilds were 'necessary' to each other, or because the Guilds would differ among themselves, seemed more facile than substantial.

In Cole's original approach to this problem there is evidence both of his Fabian background and of the influence of the then current theory of political pluralism. The great virtue of National Guild theory in his eyes was that it reconciled the opposing claims of Collectivism and Syndicalism. The sin of the former was that it found room only for the interests of the consumer; the sin of the latter that it completely ignored the interests of the consumer on the ground that producer and consumer are, or should be in a socialist society, one and the same person. Guild Socialists, on the other hand, recognised and made provision for the interests of both producer and consumer: the producer through his Guild and the consumer through the State.

The Co-Sovereignty Theory

Rejecting the doctrine of State Sovereignty which implies that the State has the ultimate right to interfere in all spheres of human action because all associations within the State ultimately derive their right to exist from the State, Cole nevertheless accepted the current Fabian theory that the State was, potentially at least, the representative of men as consumers. In a Guild Society therefore there would be, on the one hand, the grouping of men in territorial associations, the chief organ of which was Parliament, and, on the other hand, the grouping of men in vocational associations, the chief organ of which would be a Central Guilds Congress. This Guild Congress would be the supreme industrial body standing in the same relation to men as producers, as Parliament stands to men as consumers. Since both the Guild Congress and Parliament represented different types of interest, ultimate sovereignty would reside in neither body. In cases of dispute between them, however, settlement would have to be sought through a body more representative than either – a body representing every citizen in all his social aspects. The National Guild system was thus a system of co-sovereignty, resulting in a balance of powers, or, more strictly speaking, a division of powers. In the American political system, powers are divided horizontally and by stages: in the Guild system, the division would be on vertical and functional lines. The system would be one of decentralisation and dispersal of power and, in this "balancing [of] one social organism so nicely against another", the individual would find his freedom.[45]

The Civic-Sovereignty Theory

This co-sovereignty theory was criticised by the older guildsman who adhered to what they called the civic-sovereignty theory.

Hobson, the chief protagonist of the latter, rejected the Fabian idea of the State as an association of consumers. The State, he claimed, represented the interests of the citizen as distinct from those either of the producer or of the consumer, and in such a capacity must always be allowed to have the the final word in any dispute between the Guilds and the State. To Hobson, the basis of Guild organisation was the control of every economic process, productive and consumptive, so that in normal circumstances the Guilds would represent both producer and consumer. The latter he defined as "one who in his functional capacity makes an effective demand upon the producer".[46] Consumption, in his view, did not represent a homogeneous interest as Cole assumed. There was nothing between a consumer of whisky and a consumer – or 'user' and 'enjoyer' – of a municipal park which the State could represent. Production and consumption were not two distinct and equal processes but complementary stages of one economic transaction. A product was the result of co-operation between the producer and the consumer, and, once the profit motive was eliminated, there would be no divergence of interest. Provision would therefore be made inside the Guild organisation for effectual contact between producer and consumer through the establishment of a Distributive Guild to which all would belong and which would conduct negotiations, if necessary, with the manufacturing guilds.

Guild Socialism Re-stated

Among Guildsmen Cole's co-sovereignty views prevailed over Hobson's civic-sovereignty theory but the latter's criticisms led Cole to revise his conception of the consumer and consequently of the State. At the same time the influence of the early Soviet form of organisation was manifested in a further development of guild theories. In the final and most complete picture of the Guild Commonwealth which is to be found in Cole's *Guild Socialism Re-Stated*, 1920, there is a more rigorous attempt to apply the functional principle to all forms of social and industrial organisation and also a marked tendency towards decentralisation. In Hobson's original formulation of the guild system national rather than local units had been chosen because he felt that local guilds "would be altogether ineffectual and inappropriate to modem requirements".[47] This was in effect, as Penty argued, to acquiesce in the large-scale organisation, and critics had not been wanting who urged that the National Guilds would inevitably develop into highly bureaucratic bodies such as the State Departments were alleged to be. By 1920 most guildsman were prepared to admit these criticisms and, while retaining National Guilds, to agree that centralising tendencies must be opposed and that guild organisation must be highly decentralised.

Functional Democracy

The working out of the functional principle led to a rejection of the current theory of democratic representation and of the political institutions which were based on it. The present theory of political representation, it was argued, assumes that one man can represent a number of other men as men; but this assumption is unjustified. Each individual is a 'universal' with several interests and many facets to his personality. To further their various interests, each of which is more or less limited and specific, men unite in a number of associations, such as the church, the trade unions and the co-operative societies, whose 'function' is to promote those interests. A general and inclusive association such as the State claims to be cannot possibly possess a function in this sense since it is supposed to represent in an unlimited and unspecific way all men's interests, however different or divergent they may be. It is, therefore, not a 'true association'. Because no particular interest or set of interests exhausts the personality of a man, "no man can represent another man and no man's will can be treated as a substitute for, or representative of, the wills of others".[48] What it is possible to represent, concluded Cole, are not men but "certain purposes common to groups of individuals".[49] In other words, all true representation is functional in character and the democratic representative principle is not 'one man, one vote' but "one man as many votes as interests, but only one vote in relation to each interest".[50] True representative democracy, therefore, is not to be found in a single omnicompetent representative assembly such as Parliament but in a system of co-ordinated functional representative bodies. Hence, the moral to be drawn is that "the omnicompetent State with its omnicompetent Parliament ... must be destroyed or painlessly extinguished ... [for] whatever the structure of the new society may be the Guildsman is sure that it will have no place for the survival of the factotum State of today".[51]

The Withering Away of the State
Those interested in the details of Cole's blueprint of the Guild Commonwealth should read *Guild Socialism Re-Stated*. Briefly, Cole provided for four distinct forms of functional organisation: producers' guilds, consumers' councils and co-operatives, civic services, and citizens' organisations. In order that these might work as parts of a single system, there was to be a communal as distinct from a functional organisation and working of guild society. 'Communes' would need to be established at three levels – local, regional and national. The National Commune would not, however, be an extension of the present political State, nor would the local communes be extensions of the existing local authorities since these are non-functional in character and the Commune is essentially a body on which functional organisations are represented for the purposes of co-ordination. "The coordinating body which is required cannot be, in any real sense, historically continuous with the present State, and it must not reproduce in any important respect the structure of the present State".[52] Echoing Engels' famous prophecy, Cole opined that the present political machine, losing its economic and civic functions to new bodies, would "wither away".

Cole's vision of the Guild Commonwealth was criticised by the advocates of the civic-sovereignty theory who maintained that he had destroyed the State only to create a new State representative of all the major interests of society. Others, such as Carpenter, argued that the Commune would have the substance if not the form of sovereignty to which Cole was in theory so much opposed.

Whatever the force of these criticisms, it is, however, clear that Cole's *intention* was to delineate a society in which the communal power which existed would be widely dispersed. Moreover, the powers that he assigned to the communes would originate from the functional units that composed them, and the exercise of these powers, when it was necessary, would not have been felt as a purely *external* force in the way that Parliament's powers over subordinate groups are now felt. Cole's Guild Commonwealth was, in fact, much nearer to the federalist society envisaged by the anarchists than it was to the Fabian Collectivist State. Certainly, in response to the growing anti-statism in the movement, the objects of the National Guilds League were altered at its 1920 conference from: "The abolition of the Wage-System, and the establishment of Self-Government in Industry through a system of National Guilds working in conjunction with the State" to "working in conjunction with other democratic functional organisations in the Community".

Guild Socialist Prospects

Cole's re-statement of Guild Socialism marked the furthest development of guild theories. At the time of its publication the guildsmen appeared to have succeeded in displacing the old-fashioned Fabians as the acknowledged leaders of socialist thought in this country. Several of the most prominent Fabians of the pre-war days had been either converted to the new philosophy or forced to compromise with it. The only serious opposition to the intellectual plane came not from the right-wing socialists but from the small and vociferous band of Marxists. Had the National Guilds League been seeking merely to replace the Fabian Society as the centre of socialist policy-making, its prospects in 1920 would have seemed very bright, for it embraced a large number of the best publicists and the most prominent socialist intellectuals of the day. However, the very nature of Guild Socialist doctrines set the League a more difficult task than had faced the Fabians. The principal object of the latter had been to permeate with 'socialist' ideas the people who 'really mattered' – the legislators, the local councillors, the administrators, and the trade union officials and Labour leaders – those who, on the Fabian plan, would be chiefly responsible for the introduction and administration of the Collectivist State. The objects of the League, on the other hand, could not be achieved thereby. Guild Socialism could be effective only if it won the allegiance of the mass of the trade union world – the people who alone could make industrial democracy a reality. In this connection the movement had made substantial progress during the war years, especially among the shop stewards and the workshop committees. In this field, the petering out of the syndicalist movement had been a gain to guild socialism, since a number of the former syndicalists, notably John Paton, transferred their loyalties to the new movement. In addition, guild socialism could claim a substantial following among the official leaders of several of the larger trade unions, especially those in the coal mining and railway industries and in the postal services. Nevertheless, for a movement which staked so much on the conversion of the trade unions, it was a sign of weakness that the membership of the League, like that of the Fabian Society, was concentrated so much in London: in the trade union world, the centre of gravity lay in the North, not in the Metropolis.

Conflicts with the Movement
This weakness began to manifest itself after the Bolshevik Revolution in Russia. The same factors which had undermined the syndicalist movement served to undermine the guild socialist movement. The attention of the militant trade unionists – chiefly the shop stewards – began to be diverted from the economic to the political plane. The struggle against the extension of conscription and for a negotiated peace occupied more and more attention. When the conclusion of the war resolved these issues, a deeper and more significant one came to the fore. The influence of the Bolshevik Revolution was not to be confined to the utopian drawing office but was to extend to the realm of revolutionary tactics. The question was now raised: Could the reconstruction of society on guild lines proceed without the prior seizure of political power by the proletariat? To a number of the more influential guildsmen the experience of Russia demanded a negative answer.

With the thought of offering the guild idea as their contribution to the building of a Communist society after the transference of power from the ruling to the working class had taken place, they began to regard themselves as Communists first and Guildsmen second. When the CPGB was founded in 1920, they – including Ellen Wilkinson, Hobson, R.P. Dutt, Page Arnot and William Mellor – hastened to join the new organisation.

However, an important section within the League, mainly the more religious-minded, including Penty, Tawney, Reckitt and Bechhofer, strenuously resisted the Communist arguments. In April 1920, *The Guildsman* reported a crisis within the League: the Communists who believed that a sharp break with the existing order was imminent and that guild ideas could be applied only after the revolution; the constitutionalists who rejected the idea of a catastrophic and violent upheaval and saw guild socialism as primarily a method of industrial organisation; and, finally, the small centre party, led by G.D.H. and Margaret Cole, who, while sympathetic towards the Bolsheviks, were not prepared to subordinate guild socialism to any political party.[53] The differences within the League found expression at its annual conferences and finally came to a head in January 1921, when six of the right-wing members of the executive resigned protesting that the organisation had "gone Bolshevik".

Social Credit

A further factor which helped to undermine the movement was the espousal by *The New Age* of the Douglas Social Credit schemes. Orage had always remained somewhat aloof from the activities of the League itself and, as the war progressed, he became increasingly unsympathetic towards the syndicalist element in guild doctrines. From the experience of the Bolshevik Revolution, he and his immediate circle concluded that the workers were not capable of managing the larger industries themselves, at least until they had undergone a long process of technical education. When, therefore, in 1919 he added to his long list of 'editorial discoveries' the name of Major C.H. Douglas who claimed to have found that, not property but money and the manipulation of money was the root of the social evil, Orage was ready to champion the new cause with all his accustomed verve. Although Social Credit theories were at first given a guild flavour, they were in certain respects fundamentally opposed to guild doctrines. The general thesis put forward by Douglas was that industrial democracy could never be achieved so long as 'finance' remained untouched and that the important point was not workers' control of industry or even the common ownership of the means of production but the control of credit power by the consumer. It was too much to expect that the majority of guildsmen would accept this new interpretation of 'economic democracy'. The 1920 conference of the League turned down the Social Credit proposals by a large majority, further resignations and secessions took place on this score, and, henceforward, Douglas and Orage pursued their new course apart from the movement.

The Building Guilds

At the same time as differences within the Guild Socialist movement were making themselves felt, the energies of a large number of guildsmen were diverted into what proved to be an unfortunate attempt at 'propaganda by experimentation'. In an effort to redeem its wartime promises of 'homes fit for heroes', the Government, early in 1920, initiated a housing scheme under which the Treasury was to meet the residual cost of all houses built by local authorities with the aid of a fixed contribution from local rates. The first result of this scheme was to force up the price of houses to a record high level: the private builders and suppliers of builders' materials quickly realised that the local authorities had no incentive to economy and could pass on all losses to the national exchequer. In these circumstances, the local Federations of Building Trades Operatives in Manchester and London, inspired by Malcolm Sparkes, a former master builder and a Quaker socialist, offered to undertake housebuilding for the Government on a non-profit-making basis. They proposed that Building Guilds should be formed to undertake contracts on a cost-price basis plus a percentage to cover overhead expenses and a fixed allowance to enable them to grant the workers whom they employed 'continuous pay'. Working capital was to be borrowed on the security that the banks would receive the sums coming in from local authorities as the houses were built. In effect, the proposals amounted to a scheme for the establishment of Producer Co-operatives in the building industry, the main differences between the new guilds and the existing co-operative co-partnerships being that the former were to be more closely linked with the trade unions and that there was to be no form of profit-sharing.

National Guild Council

The scheme captured the imagination of many trade unionists in the building industry. A start was soon made and rapidly the Building Guild movement spread from Manchester and London to other parts of the country.[54] By December 1921 there were upwards of one hundred Building Guilds in existence and, in addition, a number of guilds in other industries – furnishing, clothing and engineering. At the suggestion of the trade unions, the local Building Guilds were later consolidated into one body, the National Building Guilds, which was registered as a limited company with a nominal capital of £100. Its headquarters were in Manchester and its leading personality was S. G. Hobson – the original National Guildsman. To facilitate the spread of the guild idea among trade unionists an offshoot of the League was formed – the National Guild Council – representative of the building and other guilds and a number of interested trade unions.

During the first eighteen months of the experiment, everything seemed to be going well. With the price of building so high and the output of labour in the building industry generally so low, the trade union workers employed by the Guild had little difficulty in providing the local authorities with better service than was being given by most private firms – at a lower cost. By the summer of 1921, however, the period of post-war inflation was coming to an end. The Government felt that in the new circumstances it could no longer afford the high prices it was paying for houses; the former method of subsidy was replaced by a fixed subsidy which left local authorities to meet a larger share of the bill for houses; and the 'cost plus' contracts were abolished in favour of 'maximum sum' contracts under which the contractors could charge costs and an overhead percentage only up to a fixed total. In addition, the conditions of interim payments to contractors for work in progress were revised so that, henceforth, a much larger working capital was needed to carry out the same amount of work.

Government Sabotage
These changes could hardly have been better designed if they had been intended – which, of course, the Government protested they were not – to sabotage the Building Guild. The Co-operative Wholesale Society's Bank which had hitherto provided the Guild's working capital refused further advances for what was now a highly speculative business. Desperately short of working capital, the Guild was forced to seek accommodation from a private bank and to entreat the building trade unions to help them by imposing a levy on their members. The National Federation of Building Trade Operatives did in fact agree to make such a levy but the response from its constituent unions was poor. The Federation was highly critical of the central management of the Guild and, when further pressed for aid, retorted that it was not a trading body but a trade union and as such could neither risk its members' money nor accept responsibility for the Guild's affairs. The Guild's finances went from bad to worse and by the end of 1922 the bank had foreclosed and the Guild was in the hands of the receivers.

The chronic shortage of working capital in its last year was undoubtedly a major cause in the collapse of the Building Guild movement but it was not the only one. In the slump conditions of 1921-22 many building trade operatives were thrown out of work and, not unnaturally, turned to the Guild for employment. There is evidence that many of the Guild jobs were over-manned and that contracts were undertaken at unduly low prices in order to keep members at work. The principle of 'continuous pay' – the Guild's most striking modification of the wage-system – aggravated the situation and diminished the competitive power of the Guild in a period of falling prices. In addition, the lack of trained managers and technicians, which had not been so important during the boom years was sorely felt under the new conditions. Hobson was inclined to blame the Guild workers themselves for lack of discipline. "In one case", he alleged,[55] "a Guild committee barely begun on a public contract, authorised a full week's pay for men to attend the local race meeting"– and to insist on the need for central control over the local bodies. Others, with some show of justice, felt that Hobson himself could not be cleared of the charge of gross mismanagement. Staking everything on a sensational success, he was mainly responsible for the Guild taking on more work at a time when it would have been prudent to reduce the scale of operations. In retrospect, it seems clear that it was a mistake to apply to a Guild operating within the framework of a capitalist society the methods and organisation which had been proposed for a fully developed guild society. Guildsmen themselves had pointed out that the Building Guilds were not Guild Socialism and that for the workers involved they were only a partial escape from 'wage-slavery'. Had the local guilds not been absorbed in the National Guild it would not have been possible to finance, by separate local action, the volume of work which central organisation made possible, but operations would have been placed on a sounder footing and it is probable that a number of them would have survived the slump. At it was, the more efficient local bodies were swamped in the disaster which overtook the national body.

The collapse of the Building Guild movement presaged the collapse of the wider movement. The initial success of the building guilds undoubtedly brought guild doctrines before a wider audience and had their success continued the Guild Socialist movement might have survived the schisms due to policy differences. In the event, their failure, which had resulted in many hundreds of operatives losing their savings, produced a reaction in the trade union movement against Guild Socialism itself. Some attempts were made to revive the building guilds on a local basis but without success. A final effort to rally the now scattered and diminished forces round the National Guild Council, into which the League had been merged in June 1923, met with the same fate. The Council declined rapidly and by the end of 1924 there was no longer a separate and organised guild socialist movement.

The Contribution of Guild Socialism

The Guild Socialist movement in its progress from the stillborn Gilds Restoration League, with its demand for the emancipation of the craftsman, to the full-blown 'functional democracy' of *Guild Socialism Re-Stated* was above all a moral revolt: a moral revolt, on the one hand, against a system of society which seemed to the guildsmen to treat the mass of people as something less than human, and, on the other hand, against an ideal – Collectivist State Socialism – which placed the amelioration of the physical condition of the people and the efficiency of the social machine above the age-long demand for freedom. In retrospect, much might be said in criticism of their passion for constitution-making, their theorising, and their 'utopianism'. But it is this element of moral revolt which remains most impressive and most enduring. The important differences that the guildsmen had with State Socialists over the organisation of industry and services in a socialist society were not so much differences about the structure of the machine as about the purposes for which it was intended. The great quarrels of mankind are not about technicalities or about the virtues of this or that form of administration, but about social values. The guildsmen left one in no doubt as to what came first in their scale of values: freedom was placed high above physical well-being and social efficiency. As Cole put it in a memorable phrase: "Poverty is the symptom: slavery is the disease ... The many are not enslaved because they are poor, they are poor because they are enslaved".[56] Men, he argued, have a right to freedom whatever they may make of it, for "the one thing that supremely matters is the free exercise of human will".[57] As for Hobson, "if it came to a choice", he said, "between industrial democracy and efficiency – an alterative I do not for one moment admit – my unequivocal choice is for democracy".[58] To Ivor Brown it appeared that the State Socialists had made the great mistake of putting socialism on a *business* instead of on a *working* basis. What he valued in the guild idea was that it had forced men to undertake a revaluation of their ideals and to ask themselves whether what they wanted was the collectivist-efficiency-leisure State dear to the followers of Webb and Wells, or the work State of William Morris.[59] Granted the Guild Socialist scale of values, it becomes clear that industrial organisation, as Cole pointed out, must be regarded as an art rather than as a science and an art whose object is not simply the production of commodities but "the production of good commodities by free men under democratic conditions".[60]

Industrial Freedom

Historically, the movement played a large part in destroying the model of the Collectivist State fashioned by the pre-1914 Fabians and, in so doing, helped to pave the way, ironically enough, for a new type of industrial organisation – the Public Corporation. But its most lasting achievement lay, as may be expected, not in the field of practice but in the realm of ideas. The Guild Socialist movement helped to popularise the idea of industrial democracy, sought to clarify its nature and provided men with an ideology of industrial freedom. Long after the details of the guild socialist blue-prints have faded in men's minds, the concept of industrial freedom which they championed – the idea of free men participating freely and fraternally in the ordering of their working lives – remains. The movement itself might die but henceforth no socialist could afford to neglect paying tribute – or, alas, more frequently, lip-service – to the ideal of industrial democracy.

Guild Socialism and Syndicalism

One last comment may be vouchsafed the historian. Guild Socialism was not merely the British equivalent – or what amounts to much the same thing, the middle-class version – of syndicalism.

It was more than that and it was this 'more' which gave it much of its charm and attracted to the movement many who would otherwise have passed it by. But it was the syndicalist content in guild doctrines which appealed most strongly to the rank and file socialists and trade unionists who joined the movement. Syndicalism proper, in this country at least, was exclusively a working class movement. Its theories, in comparison, were crude and over-simplified; its appeal limited to the small majority of class-conscious proletarians. The Guild Socialists in taking over 'the syndicalist idea' – Workers' Control of Industry – developed it, refined it and gave it a less class-conscious and a more humanitarian character. Concepts which had been only implicit in syndicalist thought and action became explicit in the hands of the guildsmen. For example, the idea that ownership was becoming divorced from control and management and that what really mattered was not who owned but who controlled and managed is much more clearly perceived by the Guild Socialists than by the Syndicalists. This deeper insight into the nature of industrial development led directly to what is perhaps the most significant distinction between the two movements.

To many guildsmen, the virtue of Guild Socialism lay in the fact that it was a compromise between Syndicalism and Collectivism, that it sought to reconcile the differences between producers and consumers not by eliminating one or other of the two categories but by establishing a just balance or division of function between producers and consumers. Not exclusive producers' control, not exclusive consumers' control, but joint control (though not joint management) of the industrial process by both producers and consumers. It may be doubted, however, whether the syndicalists did entirely overlook the claim of the consumers or whether the guild socialist compromise would have achieved a 'just balance' between the two interests.

Of deeper significance is the difference between the syndicalist and the guild socialist attitude to 'the managerial class'. Broadly speaking, the syndicalists either ignored this 'class' or considered them to be no more than the lackeys of their capitalist masters. The guild socialists, on the other hand, were among the first to point out the importance of the recent social developments which had given rise to "a class of managers, under-managers, experts and technicians, who do an ever-increasing part of the scientific and constructive work of industry, but who are salaried servants, having normally no voice in its ultimate control and no direct interest in its profits".[61] And they were the first to make a conscious effort to win the allegiance of this class to socialism. In their manifestos to 'the salariat' they cried: It's your brains we want![62] and they assured them that their position would be better under workers' than under capitalist control. They were convinced that socialists needed to make an alliance with this new 'intellectual proletariat' if socialism was to be achieved at all. If the prognostications of James Burnham turn out to be correct and the managers become the new ruling class, the vital difference between the syndicalists and the guild socialists may have to be put in this way: Syndicalism was the revolutionary movement of the proletariat which sought to achieve the emancipation of the working class by its own unaided exertions; Guild Socialism was the movement of social revolutionaries which sought to win over to the cause of the proletariat the new ruling class of managers before they had consolidated their power.

From Control to Consultation

'Joint Control': A Compromise

Between them the syndicalist and guild socialist movements achieved the popularisation of the idea of workers' control. From being, in Sidney Webb's phrase, 'an anarchist deviation', it had become by 1920, if not a respectable idea, at least a demand to be reckoned with. It was no longer possible for parlour socialists to draw up blueprints of pink futures without making special reference to the position of the workers in the control and administration of industry.

In the period 1884-1914 the bulk of the members of the Labour and Socialist movements had conceived the Collectivist State in terms of municipal ownership of local industries and State ownership, on the Post Office model, of national industries. Under the impact of syndicalist and guild criticisms of bureaucratic State socialism this conception went into the melting pot: the Collectivist State had to be re-fashioned. In keeping with the mentality of 'moderates' of every age and clime, the moderate socialists of the First World War generation did not, however, seek to re-think their general position in the light of syndicalist criticisms: instead they sought a reconciliation between 'the new socialism' and the old fashioned collectivism. The syndicalists and guildsmen had demanded workers' control; the Fabian collectivists had advocated State control: the solution 'therefore' was joint control – the sharing of control between the workers' unions and the State. The syndicalists, as might be expected, rejected this compromise 'solution'. The guild socialists, however, were more circumspect: they rejected the notion of joint management by producers and consumers but were prepared to countenance joint control by the unions with the State, *provided* that the workers were accorded the right to appoint at least 50 % of the members of any management body that might be set up. Joint control, in this form, was seen as a possible step towards workers' control – the establishment of a fully self-governing guild for every industry.

Between 1914 and 1926 the majority of nationalisation proposals put forward by constituent organs of the Labour movement were based on the notion of joint control in one form or another. Even the Webbs, those high priests of Collectivism, pronounced in its favour. In 1920, largely under the inspiration of the Webbs, the Socialisation Commission of the reconstituted Second International published a report advocating the establishment of semi-independent public boards on which the workers were to be given tripartite representation along with the representatives of management and the consumers. Labour Party conferences began to pass resolutions in favour of nationalisation "with due arrangements for the participation in management, both central and local, of the employees of all grades" – without specifying what the 'due arrangements' were to be. Several of the larger unions, notably those in the postal, engineering, railway and mining industries where syndicalist and guild socialist doctrines had found widest support, published revised plans or model bills for the nationalisation of their own industries.

The Miners and the Sankey Commission

The most famous of all the new plans of this period was the one the Miners' Federation put before the Sankey Commission in 1919. Aided by G.D.H. Cole, the miners succeeded in making this Royal Commission a forum for the discussion of industrial democracy. Human freedom, argued Cole in his evidence, "implies, not the absence of discipline or restraint, but the imposition of the necessary discipline or restraint either by the individual himself, or by some group of which he forms, and feels himself to form, a part. If then a man must receive orders, he must, if he is to be free, feel that these orders come from himself, or from some group of which he feels himself to be a part, or from some person whose right to give orders is recognised and sustained by himself and by such a group. This means that free industrial organisation must be built on the co-operation and not merely on the acquiescence of the ordinary man, from the individual and the pit up to the larger units". Such co-operation could not be achieved by State management for "a State Department is not a group of which the ordinary man feels himself to be a part".[63]

In administrative terms, the miners' plan proposed State ownership of the industry and the setting up of a Mining Council composed of ten members appointed by the Government and ten members appointed by the Miners' Federation, with the Minister of Mines as President. In addition, there were to be divisional and pit councils, similarly constituted, and an independent advisory Consumers' Council to represent the interests of the consumers.

The weakness of this attempt at a compromise solution became clear, however, when the plan was subjected to detailed scrutiny. In the event of a clash of policy between the State and the union, whose will should prevail? If the union's, why joint control in the first place? If the State's, then the union would be in the awkward position of being a party to a policy of which it disapproved.[64]

In the event, the Government rejected the miners' plan and along with it the majority report in favour of State ownership. The Commission had served the purpose of staving off temporarily the threatened coal strike and the Government could afford to bide its time for a showdown with the miners. By the time the next commission on the mining industry was set up – the Samuel Commission of 1925-26 – the miners' union had been weakened by a series of protracted and bitter strikes and lock-outs. They abandoned the demand for a half-share in control at all levels and, instead, were prepared to accept minority representation.

Managerial Socialism

The new miners' plan of 1926, which had the backing of the Labour Party and the TUC, was overshadowed by the 'General Strike' of that year. But to the historian of industrial democracy it is of special significance. For it prefigured the development of a new nationalisation policy by the Labour movement. Bureaucratic nationalisation through State Departments on the model of the Post Office had been discarded and the compromise of 'joint control' substituted. The time had now come for the abandonment of the joint control policy and with it any attempt to meet the demands of the industrial democrats. The new socialism was to be managerial socialism and its administrative form was to be the Public Corporation.

The full implications of Labour's new nationalisation policy did not become clear until the 1930s. It was not obvious at first that the Public Corporation as an administrative form could not be combined with. if not joint control, at least some element of workers' representation on the governing boards. When Morrison, the leading protagonist of the Public Corporation in Labour circles. put forward his bill for the re-organisation of London Transport in 1929, he consequently touched off a prolonged debate in the Labour movement over the question of workers' representation. This debate, as it was pursued at Labour Party Conferences and Trades Union Congresses, revealed how hazy were most of the participants' ideas of industrial democracy. No distinction was made between workers' control, joint control, and workers' representation; and it was never clearly stated who should appoint the workers' 'representatives' and to whom they were to be responsible. The appointment of a few Trade Union nominees to governing boards was frequently dubbed as tantamount to syndicalism – despite the fact that Sidney Webb had advocated it as long ago as 1891. With no organised syndicalist or guild movement to rebut such travesties, it is not surprising that the debate ended in confusion – each side claiming the victory. In retrospect, however, it is clear that the laurels went to Morrison and the advocates of managerial socialism.

The TUC and the Control of Industry

In 1932, as its contribution to the debate, the TUC published a report on the Control of Industry. This neglected report is perhaps the most important single document for the comprehension of modern Labour policy on this subject. The crux of socialisation, argued its authors, lies in the transfer to the community of *control*, not as is commonly thought of *ownership*. In the past control was automatically vested in the owners of property but this control has been successively limited by government regulation. Moreover, the increase in the scale of industrial organisation has led to the divorce of ownership from control, while at the same time ownership has come to mean not so much the ownership of tangible property as the right to receive an income in the shape of profits and interest. With the introduction of dividend limitation, this general tendency is carried a stage further until the logical conclusion is reached when the private ownership of capital seems almost meaningless, apart from the right to an annual income. In such circumstances, it is merely a matter of convenience whether socialisation takes the form of compensating the owners by the issue of Government Stock or by the issue of Public Corporation Stock. In either case, the former owners *as such* have no part in the control and management of the concern.

It can hardly have been more clearly stated that the difference between 'socialisation' *à la* Public Corporation and 'advanced capitalism' is practically indiscernible! But this was not all. The authors proceeded to subject the 'vague dogma' of workers' control to critical scrutiny. Needless to say, the upshot of their examination was that the workers had no right to control industry: all they could reasonably claim was to 'participate' in control. The workers, through their unions, had the right to influence those who did control and this could be achieved by joint consultative machinery, but they should not challenge managerial prerogatives. The determination of policy on technical, administrative, commercial and financial matters was outside the competence of the workers. "The task of business administration in this technical and commercial sense is a matter nowadays of expert training and experience. It is as much the manager's 'craft' to be able to organise the factors of production as it is the worker's 'craft' to use a lathe or a pick. It would therefore seem that efficient results can only be obtained if the final responsibility for these technical questions is left to those whose training and experience fits them for the job".[65]

Statutory Representation
It was not to be expected that even the bulk of Labour moderates in 1932 would swallow whole this piece of blatant advocacy of managerialism. Morrison's antagonists refused to yield: they insisted that in any future act of nationalisation the workers should, as a statutory right, have a number of representatives on the governing boards of the Public Corporation. The managerialists gracefully accepted the point. In 1935 the Labour Party and the TUC jointly agreed on the principle of statutory representation: the workers were to have an unspecified number of 'representatives' on the proposed boards, 'representatives' appointed by the Minister and paid by the corporation, 'representatives' who would cease to be members of their unions, 'representatives' who would be responsible not to the workers but to the Government!

Ten years later, on the eve of the election of the 1945 Labour Government, the TUC reiterated its arguments on the position of management *vis-à-vis* the workers, stating even more clearly the case against any form of the concessions that could be made to industrial democracy.[66]

In the summer of 1945 the Labour Party and the National Union of Mineworkers held joint discussions out of which emerged a detailed plan on which the Labour Government later based its Coal Industry Nationalisation Bill. In the course of these discussions, the NUM agreed that the principle of statutory representation should be dropped and that no explicit provision should be made to include on the boards of nationalised industries representatives of the workers in those industries. Thus, on the eve of realising their fifty years old demand for nationalisation, the miners – or rather, the miners' leaders – abandoned the last vestige of the syndicalist dream of 'the mine for the miners'.

The Tradition Survives

Labour Nationalisation

The 1945-51 Labour Government's nationalisation measures were constructed according to the canons of managerial socialism which Morrison and Citrine had adumbrated in the 1930s. Industrial Democracy was equated with joint consultation and managerial prerogatives were left unchallenged. All the nationalisation statutes stipulated that one of the qualifications for appointment to the new public boards was experience in labour organisation but this provision merely implied that a number of the 'safer' Trade Union officials could be offered top-level jobs in the industries: 'responsible' Labour leaders were not to be barred from entering the managerial class!

It is now clear that nationalisation has not been the panacea that its advocates predicted: the status of the workers has not been materially altered by the change from private to State ownership. In some respects conditions have improved, in others deteriorated; but the workers are still alienated from the instruments of production; they remain an inferior class within the productive process.

Inevitably there has been, within Labour-Socialist circles, a reaction to this situation. On the right-wing, nationalisation has been soft-pedalled; on the left-wing, criticisms have been made of the administrative set-up. Generally speaking, however, these criticisms have been oddly defensive in tone, while the positive proposals reveal an extreme naivety. Typical has been the demand voiced by several unions, notably the NUR, for more trade unionists on the public boards: as if a few extra Citrines and Bowmans would make all the difference! The term 'workers' control' has been bandied about but there has been little evidence that the wordspinners understood what they were talking about: it remains only an expression of discontent, not a positive demand. G.D.H. Cole, forlornly hoping for a revival of guild doctrines, has made some trenchant criticisms of the public corporations and some Fabianlike proposals for achieving the end to which he devoted his early years. But his words have been treated as no more than an echo from a distant past. The new generation of Fabian intellectuals simply shake their heads: such nonsense is not for them. Like Hugh Clegg, they make a gesture of sympathy and turn to more 'practical' matters. Workers' control might be satisfactory in a small-scale society but is not a realistic alternative for a society such as ours.[67]

The UPW

At the present times, therefore, workers' control, in the sense that I have been using the term, remains an aspiration of 'the socialist sects'. The single exception is perhaps the Union of Post Office Workers. This union, formed by amalgamation in 1920 largely owing to the inspiration of the Guild Socialists, still adheres officially to the guild objective which was written into its constitution in 1922. Alone among the larger unions, it has conducted a battle against the socialism of the public corporation. In the 1930s and again in the immediate post-war years, it made proposals for 'joint control' (Union and State) of the service as a step towards the ultimate aim. As the union with the longest experience of nationalisation, one might have thought that our Labour-Socialists, who pride themselves on their 'empiricism', would have taken some notice. Instead, the TUC looked askance at this inconvenient demand and, discouraged by lack of support from the Post Office Engineers, the UPW have not pressed the matter again.

Communist Party Opportunism

Of 'the socialist sects', the two that have shown most sympathy towards the concept are the ILP and the anarchists. The British Communist Party – more truly a sect than either – has not been included. The Communist Party attitude towards workers' control, like its attitude to all things save the Moscow party line, has been notoriously ambiguous. In its early years the Communist Party attracted to its ranks a number of prominent ex-syndicalists and, as a consequence, included 'workers' control', as one of its slogans. With the development of managerial socialism in the Soviet Union, however, the party began to change its tune. In the early 1930s the slogan was still used but it was given a new interpretation. Instead of implying the control by the workers of the enterprises in which they worked, it was taken to mean control of industry by the workers *as a class*. In this way the slogan was given a *collectivist* twist which it had not possessed before and, of course, in practice the Communists understood by workers' control of industry, the control of industry by the self-styled *party* of the working class – the Bolshevik mandarins themselves. In Britain such opportunism has led nowhere and the Communist Party can offer in its 'British Road to Socialism' nothing better on this subject than the demand for more 'workers' representatives' on management boards.

The ILP and Workers' Control

The ILP advocacy of workers' control, in contrast has been much more sincere, especially since the party ceased to be a force in the political arena. In the early 1920s the Guild Socialists almost but not quite succeeded in writing guild objectives into the ILP programme. After the party had disaffiliated from the Labour Party, its 'revolutionary' tendencies became more marked. The clearest statement of its new position was made perhaps at its Jubilee Conference in 1943. The acid test of socialisation, the party declared, was whether control was in the hands of the workers. Workers' control was "the only final and lasting solution to the anarchy of capitalist industry" and this was to be achieved through representative committees of workers on a local, area and national basis. All management and administrative staff were to be elected, subject to technical qualifications, by the workers themselves and *paid only as much as ordinary workers.*

Since the war, the ILP, along with radical elements from the Common Wealth organisation, have devoted a good deal of attention to the question, especially in relation to the theory of the managerial revolution. In an effort to rally support for the idea, these elements formed The League for Workers' Control in 1951 but the new movement proved abortive.[68]

Anarcho-Syndicalism

It is the anarchists, however, who have proved most faithful to the syndicalist tradition. Despite the differences between them and the 'pure' syndicalists in the pre-1914 period, it is the anarchists with their uncompromising hostility to 'political action' who can best lay claim to be the heirs of William Morris and James Connolly. On the international plane, anarcho-syndicalism as a distinct social theory was first formulated at the Congress of Revolutionary Syndicalists at Berlin in 1922 and since that date it has been perhaps the most coherent of the tendencies within the wider anarchist movement. In Britain the revival of anarchist thought during the Spanish Civil War was largely inspired by the activities of anarcho-syndicalists in Catalonia. Since 1945 considerable efforts have been made by British anarchists to propagate the theory of revolutionary industrial unionism. The small dissident anarchist group which was known as the Anarchist Federation transformed itself into the Syndicalist Workers' Federation, while certain numbers of the larger group centering round *Freedom* were responsible for the production of the paper *The Syndicalist*, 1952-53, and a number of pamphlets re-stating the anarcho-syndicalist position, the most notable of which was Philip Sansom's *Syndicalism: The Workers' Next Step*, 1951.

It cannot be claimed that these efforts have been rewarded by any marked revival of interest in workers' control on the part of the industrial workers and clearly a new step forwards will not come until the idea ceases to be confined to a few, relatively insignificant, groups. But at least the efforts provide evidence that the tradition dating from the Owenites is still alive in this country. In this matter, as in so many others, the anarchists remain guardians of the libertarian aspirations which moved the first rebels against the slavery inherent in the capitalist mode of production.

Notes

1. *Forecasts of the Coming Century*, edited by E. Carpenter, 1897, pp. 171-2.

2. Address to Trades' Unionists, 1885.

3. *Organised Labour: the duty of Trades' Unions in relation to Socialism*, 1886.

4. *Op. cit.*, 1920 edition, p. 653.

5. *Freedom*, November 1912.

6. *The Socialist Labour Party: its aims and methods*, 1908.

7. *Op. cit.*, p. 32.

8. *Ibid.*, p. 16.

9. *Ibid.*, pp. 25-26.

10. Mainwaring and Mobray provided a direct link with the Socialist League. Both were formerly contributors to *The Commonweal*.

11. Fernand Pelloutier, a French anarchist, who became the secretary and mastermind of the Bourses du Travail from which sprang effective labour organisation in France.

12. *cf.* G. Woodcock and I. Avakumovic: *The Anarchist Prince*, 1950, p. 294.

13. *The Syndicalist*, May 1912.

14. *cf. Freedom*, October 1907.

15. The question of the relationship between anarchism and syndicalism was discussed at length at the International Anarchist Congress, Amsterdam, 1907, where Malatesta and Max Nettlau led the opposition to the coalescence of the two movements. See *Freedom*, September-October 1907.

16. Eugene Burdick in his unpublished doctoral dissertation on *Syndicalism and Industrial Unionism in England until 1918*, Oxford University, 1950.

17. It consisted of twelve monthly pamphlets and was followed in September 1911 by *The Syndicalist Railwayman*, in its turn followed by *The Syndicalist*, January 1912.

18. This celebrated pamphlet was issued by The Unofficial Reform Committee, Tonypandy, 1912. According to Burdick, it was the joint product of six authors: Charles Gibbons, Noah Rees, Noah Ablett, W.F. Hay, George Dolling, and W.H. Mainwaring.

19. *From Single Tax to Syndicalism*, p. xiv.

20. This was the title of the English translation, published 1913, of their book: *How we shall bring about the Revolution*. One of the translators was Frederick Charles who had been concerned the so-called anarchist 'bomb plot' at Walsall, 1892.

21. *Syndicalism: its basis, methods and ultimate aims*, 1913.

22. Apart from these two conferences the ISEL called an International Congress which was held in London, September to October 1913. It was mostly concerned with the question of trade union structure.

23. This repudiation sometimes went so far as a repudiation of the famous syndicalist slogan itself: "Syndicalism does not hold with the position of the mines for the miners, though Syndicalists would prefer even that to the present state of affairs ... Syndicalism favours the administration of the mines for the miners on the theory that none knows as well as the miners themselves the various details connected with the mining industry". *The Syndicalist*, June, 1912.

24. *Syndicalism: what is it?*, no date.

25. 'The Genesis of Syndicalism in France', appendix to *Self-Government in Industry*, 1917.

26. W.F. Hay: *Industrial Syndicalist*, November 1910.

27. *The Syndicalist*, February 1914.

28. See *Fields, Factories and Workshops*, and *Freedom* October 1909 and March 1912.

29. See his *The Workers' Committee*, 1918.

30. i.e. W. Gallacher – John Paton, who had joined the Guild Socialists, had died in 1920.

31. My italics.

32. *The Syndicalist*, February 1914.

33. Quoted in N. Carpenter: *Guild Socialism*, 1922, p. 91.

34. *The New Age*, 30th December 1909.

35. *The New Age*, 8th January 1912.

36. See Cole and Mellor: *The Greater Unionism*, 1913.
37. *Towards a Postal Guild*, 1919.
38. M. B. Reckitt and C. E. Bechhofer: *The Meaning of National Guilds*, 1920 edition, p. 190.
39. *The Guildsman*, March 1920.
40. *Op. cit.*, pp. 3-4, 6-7.
41. Cole: *Labour and the Commonwealth*, 1918, p. 32.
42. Cole: *Guild Socialism Restated*, 1910, p. 53.
43. Cole: *Self-Government in Industry*, 3rd edition, 1929, p. 216. For a more complete picture of the working of industrial democracy, see Cole's sketch of the constitution for an Enginering Guild, *ibid.* pp. 211-229.
44. *Guild Socialism Restated*, p. 57.
45. *Self-Government in Industry*, p. 14.
46. Hobson: *National Guilds and the State*, 1920, p. 25.
47. *National Guilds*, p. 276.
48. Cole: *Social Theory*, p. 103.
49. *Ibid.*, p. 106.
50. *Ibid.*, p. 115.
51. *Guild Socialism Restated*, p. 32.
52. *Op. cit.*, p. 121.
53. Cole's attitude inspired M.B. Reckitt's triolet:
Mr G.D.H. Cole
  Is a bit of a puzzle,
A curious rôle
That of G.D.H. Cole,
With a Bolshevik soul
  In a Fabian muzzle;
Mr G.D.H. Cole
  Is a bit of a puzzle.
54. *The Guildsman*, February 1920, published the following 'announcement':
Birth – January 1919, at Manchester, Building Trade Unionists and the National Guilds League, of a Guild. Parents and child are doing well.
Marriage – January 1919, at Manchester, a marriage has been arranged

between the labour power of the building workers and the credit of the public.

Death – January 1919, at Manchester, the theory of the necessity of Capitalism passed painlessly away. No flowers by request.

55. *The Guild Socialist*, January 1923.

56. *Self-Government in Industry*, p. 110.

57. *Labour and the Commonwealth*, p. 219.

58. *National Guilds and the State*, p. 12.

59. *The New Age*, 6th May 1915.

60. *Labour and the Comonwealth*, p. 32.

61. R.H. Tawney in *The Guildsman*, June 1921.

62. *The Guild Socialist*, August 1921.

63. Coal Industry Commission, *Evidence*, Cmd. 359/1919, Vol. 1, pp. 548 ff.

64. For a 'syndicalist' critique of joint control on these lines see *A Plan for the Democratic Control of the Mining Industry*, 1919, published by the South Wales Socialist Society.

65. *TUC Report*, 1932, p. 217.

66. Report on Post-War Reconstruction, *TUC Report*, 1944, p. 411.

67. See H. Clegg: *Industrial Democracy and Nationalisation*, 1951.

68. Its publications included *Workers' Control in the Modern World* by Don Bannister and *Industry and Democracy* by the former Guild Socialist Maurice Reckitt.

Fabianism and the Managerial Revolution

(The Fabian Society has recently celebrated its 70th anniversary. Although at the outset it included anarchist as well as state socialist elements, it soon replaced any revolutionary objectives it may have avowed by the doctrine of 'the inevitability of gradualness'. In the article below an attempt is made to assess the significance of Fabianism in the light of the emergence of what James Burnham has called 'the managerial society' and to interpret the tasks of the future in the light of this assessment).

When the future historian comes to write the history of the managerial social revolution in this country, he will undoubtedly assign a prime role to the Fabians. To them belongs the credit for preparing the way for the peaceful emergence of the new ruling class by the elaboration of a 'socialist' ideology which could, at one and the same time, enlist the sympathy of the proletariat without antagonising those elements of the old capitalist class which were to be enrolled in the new ruling class of managers.

Today, as always, the membership of the Fabian Society is limited to a few thousand middle class intellectuals but the Society has never estimated its success in terms of membership figures. Its criterion of success has ever been the extent to which its ideas have permeated political parties and the Labour Movement, and, judged on this standard, no one can deny its victory. British Socialism, except for the Communist and other minor elements, is essentially Fabian Socialism.

Fabianism has sometimes been regarded as essentially a tactical method – the method of permeating other bodies with the object of furthering Fabian ends – but the superficiality of this view is obvious. Tactics presuppose doctrines and in the light of the emergence of the new social order the leading ideas of Fabianism may be characterised as follows:

First and most obvious is the rejection of the theory of the class struggle which assigns to the proletariat the chief role in the achievement of the free, classless, socialist society. The popularity of the early Fabians, as E.R. Pease, the historian of the Society has suggested, was in no small part due to their freeing British Socialism from revolutionary ideas and diverting it into constitutional paths, thereby making it respectable for even the middle class 'do-gooders' to profess a belief in socialism. The Fabian Society began and has continued as essentially a middle class movement, with middle class men and with middle class ideas and prejudices. No one will deny that the Fabians have often displayed a genuine sympathy for the poor and the oppressed, but however much they were *for* the working class they were never *of* it. To the Fabian the working class has always appeared at best as a rather stupid helpless child who requires an intelligent guardian to protect him.

The second and equally important Fabian doctrine is the acceptance of the bourgeois democratic State as a suitable instrument for the achievement and application of socialism. No essential change, the Fabians argued, was necessary, as the Marxists thought, in the apparatus of government. Much less was it necessary, as the anarchists believe, to destroy the whole conception of the modern centralised State. To break the State machine, said Shaw with a characteristic glibness, is tantamount to Luddism: "I regard machine breaking as an exploded mistake. A machine will serve Jack as well as his master if Jack can get it out of his master's hands. The 'State Machine' has its defects; but it serves the enemy well enough; and with a little adaptation, it will serve us quite as well as anything we are likely to put in its place." (*Today*, September 1887).

All that was required was for the people to gain control of the machine through the use of their votes and to perfect it for their own ends. With the acceptance of the democratic State went the tendency to identify it with the community. Such an identification made it possible to regard State control and State ownership as control and ownership by the community in the interests of 'the community as a whole'.

The Fabian rejection of the class struggle and their attitude to the State inevitably had important repercussions on their theory of socialisation. The revolutionary socialists and anarchists, grounding their theory on the prime importance of the ownership of the means of production as the source of power the ruling class, were led to draw a distinction between capitalist public ownership and genuine socialisation. The capitalists as a class, however much certain interested sections of them might be hostile to particular acts of nationalisation, were not averse to, and indeed supported, a limited extension of it in those services which were natural monopolies and which were of great importance to the functioning of private industry — notably communications, transit and power.

Such nationalisation could be welcomed as increasing the general efficiency of private industry, as providing a secure and profitable field for investment, and as producing surpluses which could be used to relieve national and local taxation on property. The extension of public ownership by a capitalist controlled State could, therefore, only mean the strengthening of capitalist domination.*

The Fabians, in contrast, showed themselves far less discriminating. Every extension of public ownership and control they welcomed as a victory for the community over the capitalists, and socialism became practically equivalent to the extension of State power and ownership. The original 'Basis' of the Society is a revealing document. Its stated object was not, as the revolutionary socialists would have put it, 'the emancipation of labour through the socialisation of the means of production', but instead 'the emancipation of land and capital from individual ownership'. This more limited object betrays the fact that the Fabians from the outset were far more markedly anti-capitalist than pro-labour.

The fourth essential Fabian doctrine was the theory of the limited role of workers' organisations in a socialist society. The acceptance of the bourgeois State machine with its location of sovereign legal

---

* This revolutionary distinction between capitalist nationalism and socialist nationalisation, however useful in the past, is now outmoded in most advanced industrial countries. Nationalisation no longer serves the interest of the capitalists and its further extension spells their extinction. The important distinction is between nationalisation, whether 'capitalist' or 'socialist', and a form of socialisation which ensures workers' control.

power in Parliament entailed the corollary that any institutions the workers built up should be subordinate to it. The early Fabians neglected to study the main working class organisations – the Trade Unions and the Co-operatives. Sidney and Beatrice Webb, however, soon made up for this deficiency and in so doing laid down the broad principles which should govern their functioning in a socialist society. Socialism, they decided, meant essentially paramount control by the consumer. Producers' co-operatives, for long the ideal of nineteenth century socialists, were ruled out as liable to be anti-social as well as being impracticable.

Consumers' co-operation naturally had a part to play in the field of distribution, but elsewhere it suffered from inherent limitations which only the State could overcome. The function of the Trade Unions was to represent the interests of the producers vis-à-vis the consumers. The extent of Trade Union control was, however, to be strictly limited to a partial control over the conditions of work. In no circumstances was it to extend to interference in the productive side of business management.

The fifth and perhaps most significant Fabian idea is the notion of the peculiar importance of experts – the administrators and the managerial elements. As one historian of socialism has so naively put it, Fabian Socialism "saw in the middle class a group that could be utilised in developing the technique of administration on behalf of the new order" (Laidler: *Socio-Economic Movements*). The early Fabians included a high proportion of upper Civil Servants and not unnaturally stressed the importance of efficient bureaucratic administration. Early Fabian literature contains no hint of the elective control of officials – a plank in the programme of the Social Democratic Federation which the latter got from Joseph Lane's Labour Emancipation League. On the contrary, officials were to be appointed from above by the State after examination, and controlled only indirectly by the community through Parliament. Pre-1914 Fabianism appears as essentially bureaucratic socialism and was attacked as such by the syndicalists and the guild socialists.

After 1918 the emphasis on political bureaucracy disappears to be replaced by a growing emphasis on the importance of the managerial elements in a socialist society – a change which coincided with the abandonment of the concept of nationalisation through a Government Department on the model of the Post Office in favour of nationalisation through semi-independent public corporations which are much less amenable to public control. But from the beginning the Fabians had not neglected to woo the managers. Accepting explicitly the development of modern large-scale industry, they underlined, as early as the *Fabian Essays* of 1889, the growing distinction between the capitalist owners and the salaried managers, the latter performing the indispensable function of organising production while the former, through their property rights, simply laid claim to profits, rent and interest. The progressive development of industry from individual ownership and management to joint stock companies and trusts indicated, they argued, that the next step, as each industry became 'ripe' for control, was the elimination of the capitalist owners, the State taking the place of the shareholders "with no more dislocation ... than is caused by the daily purchase of shares on the Stock Exchange" (Sidney Webb). The managers were further reassured by the categorical statement that there would be no nonsense about equality of wages. The Fabian Society, declared one of its tracts (No. 70, 1896), "resolutely opposes all pretensions to hamper the socialisation of industry with equal wages, equal hours of labour, equal official status, or equal authority for everyone". Management, it was later pointed out, is, or is fast becoming, a specialist technique, and its profession must be organised as such and paid its appropriate reward. (Webb: *The Works Manager Today*, 1916).

With this high regard for bureaucratic and managerial administration went a characteristic managerial ideal – that of social efficiency, an ideal, which, if it has always found expression in socialist literature, has previously been subordinate to the more human values of freedom, mutual aid and social co-operation. The Fabians above all emphasised the economic advantages to be gained from a collectivist economy – the replacement of the 'anarchy' of competition by planned production and the elimination of wasteful unemployment and poverty through the establishment of a national minimum standard of life. The total effect of Fabian doctrine was thus to transform socialism from a moral ideal of the emancipation of the proletariat to a complicated problem of social engineering, making it a task, once political power had been achieved, not for the ordinary stupid mortal but for the super-intelligent administrator armed with facts and figures which had been provided by diligent research.

Today with our retrospective wisdom, it requires no great insight to see how these five essential Fabian doctrines have contributed to the development, not of the free, classless, socialist society but of the managerial society. The rejection of the class struggle and the insistence that there could be, even in a predominantly capitalist society, a genuine community of interests, has had the effect of turning the proletariat away from its revolutionary objective and towards the goal of mere amelioration through social reforms.

The acceptance of the existing State meant the acceptance of an institution which, whilst it suited the bourgeoisie and could be, in this country at least, fairly readily adapted to the new ruling class of managers, is incapable of being controlled by the workers. The State and especially its central organs, as all who study its functioning know and as all practical politicians realise, is essentially a power over and above the people and not one readily amenable to their control. It acts in their name but in reality it acts in the interests of the dominant groups in society which control the instruments of production, however many concessions it may care to make in the way of social welfare schemes. The Fabian theory of State ownership in the interests of the community, coupled with the insistence on the subordinate role of the trade unions and co-operatives and on the importance of the experts, the bureaucrat and the manager, is one that is of direct interest to the managerial class, just as it is opposed to the interests of both the workers and (in the long run) to the capitalist owners.

No amount of assertion, statutory or otherwise, that nationalised industries are to be run 'in the public interest' can disguise the fact that they are being run in the interests of those in whom the real control is vested.

The concept of 'the public interest', in itself an unanalysable mumbo-jumbo, is in fact a beautiful ideological smokescreen to hide the interests of the managers while, at the same time, exposing the capitalists to public obloquy and confusing the workers. The limitation of the Trade Unions to a subordinate role in the nationalised industries means, moreover, that these working class organisations which could and should be operated as a base for building up, "within the womb of the old society", the power of the proletariat, have been castrated from the outset: the Trade Unions are to be used by the new masters, many of whom are ex-Trade Union leaders, only as more refined instruments for disciplining the workers. The emphatic rejection of the revolutionary idea of workers' control – the most direct threat that the managers had to face – is a signal victory for the new ruling class.

These five leading Fabian doctrines are thus all in keeping with the interests of the new ruling class that is emerging. The acceptance of them as the basis of the new social order constitutes the great illusion of our time. The application of them leads not to the free, classless, socialist society: it leads to the managerial society and the history of their application by the Labour Government serves only to underline that fact more clearly.

It may be that the managerial society is inevitable if present tendencies continue but this does not mean that the dominance of the managers must be meekly accepted. The proletarian social revolution may be further off than we once thought and the difficulties of bringing it to birth may be more substantial than we once optimistically imagined, but this provides no reason why we should not continue to work for it. To think otherwise is to accept – as Burnham himself accepts – the fallacy of historical determinism.

But we can only work for the proletarian social revolution if we have cleared our minds of the ideology of the managers. The time has now come for laying the foundations of a new workers' movement – a movement which will not be misled by doctrines that appear to hold out the prospect of workers' emancipation but in reality hands over the workers to new masters, a movement which will cut through the web that the Fabians have so cunningly spun, albeit half-unconsciously, in the interests of the managers.

In terms of the Fabian doctrines outlined above this new workers' movement must recognise :

i) That the theory – and practice! – of the class struggle must be redefined in such a way as to make clear that the proletariat has two enemies, the old, fast-disappearing capitalist class and the new increasingly powerful managerial class – the men whose social power is based not on their property rights but on the key positions which they hold within the industrial process. The long and bitter struggle of the first workers' movement is drawing to a close. The drama is ending in a Pyrrhic victory for the workers and the stage must now be set for the next and second phase of the class struggle – the struggle against the managerial class.

ii) That the State can never serve as an instrument to achieve workers' emancipation and that political action, in the narrow sense of parliamentary and party politics, is profoundly irrelevant to the real struggle – the struggle within the workshops.

iii) That nationalisation as such is no concern of the working class. It may facilitate the technical and economic reorganisation of industry – its primary purpose – and incidentally provide the means by which extra concessions can be made to the workers but it does nothing to alter their status: they remain essentially wage-slaves. Only a form of socialisation which ensures control by the workers in place of control by the managers and bureaucrats is worth pursuing.

iv) That a serious attempt must be made to build up workers' organisations with their own culture, morals and ideology, free from middle class influence. The first workers' movement failed lamentably in this respect. By diverting the struggle into political channels the middle class were able to assume control and leadership of the workers' movement. An anti-political and industrial movement provides no opportunity for the careerist and frustrated intellectual. Of the two genuinely working class forms of organisation – the trade unions and the co-operatives – the first has been content to remain a purely defensive instrument so far as industrial organisation is concerned; and when it did decide to take positive action it did so in the form of creating a political party which at once succumbed to Fabian permeation. The second – potentially the more revolutionary in that it attempts to lay hold on the means of production and distribution *directly* instead of through the State – has survived only by abandoning its ideals.

v) Lastly, the new workers' movement must face squarely the problem of controlling the expert and devise means to ensure that he remains on tap not on top. Complex modern industrial organisation cannot function without experts – men with the technical know-how which nowadays requires a long and expensive training. To talk as though the ordinary workers at the bench could tomorrow take over the functions of management, if only they had the will and the opportunity, is mere moonshine. Opposition to the managerial class does not mean opposition to management as such. Workers' control does not imply the abolition of management: it implies the control of managerial functions by the workers. Workers' control in this sense will be no easy matter to achieve but achieved it must be if the emergence of a new ruling class is to be prevented now and in the future. Workers' control is and remains the touchstone of any successful workers' revolution.

The new workers' movement, in other words, must be essentially a syndicalist movement. The nineteenth century anarchist-communist movement showed great prescience when, in opposition to Fabian and Marxist socialists alike, it predicted that state socialism would result in the exchange of one set of masters for another, but it also had its weaknesses. It underestimated the immense difficulties of organising a successful social revolution and failed to emphasise the importance of building up workers' organisations for the two-fold purpose of waging the daily struggle against capitalism and of creating the administrative units of the new society. This defect in anarchist doctrine was recognised by the pre-1914 syndicalist movement – although the rapidity with which that movement disintegrated after the Bolshevik Revolution of 1917 indicates that many syndicalists soon forgot the text which they had preached and acted upon: that no new system can supersede another until it has become fully matured within the womb of the old. Nevertheless, syndicalism of the period 1900-1920 now appears as the great heroic movement of the proletariat, the last desperate attempt before society took the plunge down the managerial abyss to emancipate the proletariat by its own exertions, to build up a distinct proletarian culture purged of any traces of bourgeois ideology, and to evolve a uniquely proletarian method of social action. To the Fabian who is constitutionally incapable of conceiving a society which is not constructed according to the canons of bourgeois architecture, syndicalism seems a crude and impractical social theory. But those who are to play their part in the new workers' movement in opposition to the managerial State will find in it the fount of their inspiration.

Industry and the Managerial Society

During the past seven or eight years a desultory debate has been going on in the Labour Movement on the subject of public ownership. Contrary to popular belief, public ownership in the sense of ownership by the State or other governmental agencies is not genetically a socialist idea. In the early nineteenth century there were advocates of municipal gas and water works and even railway nationalisers who would have been aghast at being identified with the socialists, while the socialists themselves thought of the future society in terms of *voluntary* co-operative communism. It was not until the 1880s with the virtual triumph of Marxist doctrines that socialism came to be practically identified with State ownership. The British Labourites, rejecting revolutionary methods in favour of Fabian gradualism, nevertheless adopted the Marxist formula of the nationalisation of the means of production, distribution and exchange. Adherence to this formula then became the hallmark of the 'genuine' socialist, as distinct from the 'exceptional' socialist – Liberal or Conservative in politics – who advocated nationalisation of particular industries, usually those deemed to be 'natural' monopolies. It is for this reason that 1918 is usually held to be such a significant date in the history of the Labour Party, for in that year the party adopted as one of its principal objects "the common ownership of the means of production, distribution and exchange". This phrase signified to the wider world the party's conversion from a mere social reform to a full-blooded socialist party.

The object remains written in the Labour Party's constitution and is quoted with apparent approval in the first paragraph of the new policy statement, *Industry and Society*. But for many influential Labourites the formula has lost much of its old magic. In 1945 the general talk was of "the first instalment of socialism", meaning by that the nationalisation of the basic industries, with the implication that the rest would, by the grace of God and the electorate, follow in due course. During the first four years of the Labour Government there were no serious misgivings among the leadership over the nationalisation policy but in 1949 the 'moderates' expressed doubts about steel and it is no secret that it was only the pressure of the Leftists which secured the nationalisation statute of that year. Morrison began to drop large hints about the need for time to digest the industries already swallowed and the more sophisticated started to prate about the virtues of 'the mixed economy'. This latter term particularly stank in the nostrils of the Leftists: it seemed tantamount to a repudiation of the old faith. So, for a time, the issue was raised: more nationalisation or less, and how soon?, with the Leftists of course on the side of 'progress'. Hardly a voice could be heard suggesting that what was wrong with the Labour Party was not its pace but its direction.

* * *

Then, in 1951, the Socialist International weighed in with the pronouncement that the essence of socialism was not public ownership but economic planning: public ownership was one of the techniques to be used in planning an economy but "socialist planning does not presuppose public ownership of all the means of production". Taking this as its cue, the German Social Democratic Party – that erstwhile representative *par excellence* of milk and water Marxism – has now abandoned its nationalisation objectives and has come out in favour of private, if regulated, enterprise. Its British counterpart, the Labour Party, has been more circumspect. Here the issue has been complicated by the Bevanite struggle and by the fact that the party activists, especially in middle-class constituencies, have proved to be obstinately wedded to the old faith. Conference resolutions to nationalise this, that and the other industry keep cropping up and even if the National Executive, with the aid of the block vote of the larger trade unions, can prevent them being passed, they testify to the emotive appeal of the old formula. However, not even the Leftists can pretend to be enthusiastic about the *form* nationalisation has taken in the past. Statistics 'demonstrating' the success of nationalisation cannot disguise the obvious fact that the setting up of a few public corporations in the major industries of the country has not instituted the millennium or begun to look like instituting it. For the Leftists, then, it has been a question of 'more nationalisation but' – the 'but' being followed by some asinine generality about the need for more democratic control or the suggestion that perhaps a government department on the model of the Post Office might be better than a public corporation after all.

In truth, the Leftist Labourites have in the last few years shown themselves to be pretty feeble intellectually. Their favourite Welsh Charley can spin fine phrases and take the mickey out of the hecklers but he hasn't got a new idea in his head. With the result that the clever young graduates in economics have been making circles round them with such dexterity that they have succeeded in pinning on the nationalisers the labels 'old-fashioned' and 'reactionary'. 'The New Socialists' have produced provocative and weighty books like the Socialist Union's *Twentieth Century Socialism* and Crosland's *The Future of Socialism*, while all that their opponents have managed to muster is an odd pamphlet or two and Strachey's *Contemporary Capitalism* – the latter with its Marxist overtones being so much to the point that its author has publicly acknowledged that no policy conclusions are to be derived from it!

* * *

The New Socialists have not only mastered Keynesian economics; they have also been reading Burnham and some of the modern sociologists. From the latter they have learned that social inequalities are buttressed by institutions other than private property, our educational institutions in particular. Hence the importance attached by recent Labour thought to education reform and the comprehensive school. From Burnham, they have learned the importance of the distinction between ownership and the control of industry. True, this distinction was not first drawn by Burnham. It was implicit in classical syndicalist thought before World War One and was made explicit by the Guild Socialists. Also, it underlay the arguments in the TUC's important report on *The Control of Industry*, 1932, which decisively repudiated industrial democracy in favour of joint consultation. But it was Burnham who gave the idea wide currency by linking it with a dramatic revision of Marx's theory of social change. By and large, Labourite intellectuals did not begin to take Burnham seriously until several years after 1945: if they had done so, they might have been less enthusiastic about the party's nationalisation programme. It was only when, for other reasons, doubts began to arise concerning the efficacy of nationalisation that Burnham was brought into the picture.

Burnham's general analysis may, according to one's temperament and objectives, be interpreted in either a radical or a conservative way. To the syndicalist, for example, the decline in the importance of the functions of ownership reinforces the arguments in favour of workers' control. If capitalist control is on the way out, it becomes an urgent necessity, if a new ruling class is not to emerge, for the workers to assume control of the instruments of production. But suppose one is not seriously worried about the idea of a ruling class, so long as it is not called by that name; suppose one is not prepared to forgo any of the advantages of large scale and mass production which requires for its organisation a professional elite of managers; suppose, even, that one sees a fair prospect that in the future set-up one has a chance of becoming a member of the new power elite; why, then, Burnham's analysis appears in a quite different light! Of course, one must avoid mentioning Burnham: the name is slightly odoriferous; and in 1942 when *The Managerial Revolution* was first published Burnham was still something of a radical – he didn't in so many words actually approve his predictions and a critical reader, not weighed down by his pseudo-deterministic fallacy, might well draw the 'wrong' conclusion; that efforts should be made to halt the march of the managers. The conservative, therefore, must tread gingerly: his best course is to steal Burnham's leading ideas and to dress them up in a manner more appealing to the popular palate.

This, roughly, is what the authors of *Industry and Society: Labour's Policy on Future Public Ownership* have done. On any reckoning this statement is a landmark in the development of British socialist thought. Despite the evidence it contains of a carefully contrived compromise designed to satisfy both the New

Socialists and the Leftists, it is an intelligent and persuasive document. It has been and will be attacked by the Leftists but mostly for the wrong reasons; some of Labour's leading capitalists, like R.R. Stokes and Sir Hartley Shawcross, may object when – or if – its ideas are put into practice; but I shall be very surprised if it is not accepted with anything more than a murmur of protest by the dissident rank and file at the next Annual Conference of the Party in October.

* * *

A large part of *Industry and Society* is devoted to an analysis of recent changes in the structure of industry. In the last forty years the pace of technological change has quickened, a new pattern of production has emerged, mass production has increased, and the tendency towards amalgamation has continued. As a consequence we have witnessed the emergence of the large firm to a position of dominance in the economy. The number of joint stock companies – now some 291,000 – has increased but the great bulk of these are small 'private companies' with fifty or less shareholders. The number of 'public companies' – those permitted to raise money on the capital market – has however declined to a figure of just over 11,000. It is these public companies which really count. Their total paid up capital of £4,340 million is nearly twice that of all private companies and, measured in terms of the value of their shares, public companies account for 80% and private companies 20% of total company wealth. Within the class of public companies a further group can be distinguished: that of some 500 firms, each with assets in excess of £2½ million. It is this group of super-firms which accounts for nearly 50% of the profits made by private industry. As Peter Drucker noted in *The New Society*, it is the super-firm which is the decisive institution in our economy: "The great majority of people do not work for the large industrial enterprises yet their livelihood is directly dependent upon them ... The enterprise determines economic policies and makes economic decisions. A small number of big enterprises sets the wage pattern and establishes the 'going wage' of the economy".

The super-firm is ostensibly a capitalist institution: it is owned by private individuals and corporate shareholders. But – and this is the point – it is run by its managers. In the words of the policy statement: "As companies grow larger and their affairs more complex, management becomes increasingly important, increasingly specialist and increasingly professional. More and more it assumes a life of its own. In the large companies it is the managers who now undertake the functions once performed by capitalist owners". It is an exaggeration to say that the functions of management are completely divorced from the functions of ownership or that the interests of the managers and those of the shareholders are necessarily conflicting. But undoubtedly the managers do think and behave differently from the capitalists. "The world of the managers is not the world of the shareholders. Their concern is with production as much as with profits and with expansion far more than with dividends. Salaries, pensions, status, power and promotion – these rather than wealth are their operating incentives". The tensions reflected in the formation of shareholders' associations and the recent 'take-over' bids serve only to underline these truths. The fragmentation of ownership – the reduction in size and the increase in the number of shareholdings – contributes to building up the effective power of the controlling managers *vis-à-vis* the capitalist owners. By and large the managers are not themselves substantial shareholders in the concerns they control and to an increasing extent these firm are self-financing. The capital required for further expansion is provided from profits rather than distributed in the form of larger dividends, with the result that dependence on the shareholder is further reduced. 'The profit motive' still operates, of course, but the dividend is not the dominant impulse. "Company aggrandisement, conceptions of the national interest, prestige and power, pensions and pay for chief executives – these are now the main incentives for those on their way up and for those who have arrived in the Board Room".

Historically, the 'justification' of the capitalist's existence has been couched in terms of his risk-bearing function – he risks his capital in return for a chancy dividend. This 'justification' still applies in the small firm and in a competitive industry the risks to capital may be quite high. But it no longer applies to the thousands of owners of the large firm. The ICIs and Unilevers of this world never find themselves in Carey Street. Such firms never go bankrupt, they could not be allowed to fail: their prosperity in fact is "now substantially underwritten by the State". With the decline in the capitalist's risk-bearing function, with the possibility of accumulating capital within the company itself, and with the emergence of a professional class of managers, any case for retaining the capitalist goes by the board. These super-firms could be run without owners and one notable German firm – the Volkswagen company – is in fact so run, as was the Steel Company of Wales during its period of 'suspended ownership', following de-nationalisation.

The shareholders of the super-firms, of course, retain certain 'rights', above all the 'right' to receive the greater part of the new wealth created by economic expansion: their shares increase in value as the firms grow and more than keep pace with increases in the cost of living. But, with the whittling away of his social functions, this 'right' becomes increasingly merely a barefaced privilege – a parasitic claim on the efforts of the producers, a claim that could be rejected without leading to any problem of operation and management.

All this is familiar to the student of industrial organisation, although many socialists – and anarchists – still talk as if we were living in a nineteenth century capitalist economy. What, then, does the Labour Party propose to do with these five hundred super-firms?

It is at this point that the conservatism of the authors asserts itself. If control is now largely in the hands of the managers, one might expect the socialists to transform them into real public companies, i.e. the State would take over *both* the ownership *and* control of their assets. But nothing so simple or straightforward emerges. Instead, 'the community' is invited to become the owners of industrial shares. How? Through the investment in equity shares of the fund to be established as a consequence of the party's National Superannuation proposals; through death duties being paid in shares and land as well as in cash; and (to be more precise!) through "other methods and other agencies". When? The reader may fix his own date because the authors studiously avoid giving any. There is only the broad hint that "it is not our intention that the Government should indulge in a wildly inflationary scramble for shares: both the timing and occasion for acquiring shares will need careful consideration". This is Sidney Webb's 'inevitability of gradualness' with a vengeance!

Through its participation in shareholding, 'the community', i.e. the State (our authors, of course, equate the two) secures for itself the rewards hitherto claimed by the private capitalist. Thereby "a fairer distribution of income and wealth" is achieved – provided that the controllers of the State see fit.

So, the State becomes (gradually) the owner or part-owner of public companies. But our analysis has already shown that ownership is virtually divorced from control. What happens under the new dispensation to the controlling power of the managers? Answer: it stays, more or less, where it is. The case for control is, we are told, quite distinct from the case for ownership. General controls over the super-firms and industry generally there will be, for the sake of securing a measure of central planning. Just what these controls will mean in practice we are not told but are referred to a future policy statement on the subject to be published next year. We may safely assume, however, that they will be similar to the general controls exercised by the Government in war-time and by the post-war Labour Government, with perhaps less emphasis on direct controls and more inducement controls – financial baits and the like. What such general controls will *not* mean is close supervision of the managers: "The Labour Party recognises that, under increasingly professional managements, large firms are as a whole serving the nation well ... No organisation, public or private, can operate effectively if it is subjected to persistent and detailed interventions from above. We have, therefore, no intention of intervening in the management of any firm which is doing a good job".

But what of 'the problem of public accountability'? Students of public administration, to say nothing of the general public, have been much concerned about the irresponsibility of the public corporations which run the nationalised industries. On this particular question another policy statement, *Public Enterprise*, recommends only a few minor changes which will leave the problem where it is. But the public corporations are statutory bodies over which the Government and Parliament have, in theory, considerable control. If there is a problem of public accountability in respect of public corporations, how much more will there be one in respect of the proposed semi-public forms. The authors of *Industry and Society* don't altogether ignore the problem. They recognise that "the Boards of large firms are almost wholly autonomous. They exercise enormous power without being responsible to anybody. They may exercise that power well, but it is hardly satisfactory that there should be no accountability whatever". At this point the reader should prepare himself for one of those asinine generalities which are a substitute for hard thinking in Labour circles. "It is possible", we are told, "that the best way of dealing with this situation is to review the Companies' Act and to develop more definite forms of public accountability. The essential point is that the Boards of these companies should conduct their affairs in a manner which coincides with the interests of the community."

Perhaps conscious that these supine observations will receive the scorn they merit, the authors have added another section dealing with this general problem of control of the managers. Its title is promising: The Problem of Social Power. Its third sentence even reads: "From existing Board Room policies it is not difficult to envisage a managerial caste taking on the former role of the owners of wealth and using its economic power to buttress class privileges and institutions". Good! Nay, excellent! The possibility of the managerial revolution is acknowledged, even if Burnham isn't. Let us hear, and right soon, the answer we've all been waiting for!

We are informed, quite correctly, that in recent years privilege in its many forms has been financed increasingly from company resources and decreasingly from private savings. This follows naturally from the increase in personal taxation of the rich and the decrease in shareholders' unearned income, on the one hand, and from the ability of companies to accumulate financial resources and to secure favourable tax treatment of business expenditure, on the other. The managers today don't pay for their privileges like the capitalists did and do: they get their companies to pay for them. Expense accounts, cars, meals, travel, entertainment, holidays, 'top-hat' pension schemes, the provision of houses and servants, interest-free loans, help with school fees and the like – all these are ways in which the managers, as distinct from the capitalists, secure the rewards of being the men who control the instruments of production. These privileges are acquired by being a member of the managerial élite: they serve the dual function of being perks for the boys, for 'the top people', and also of being a handy method of controlling any individual manager or would-be manager who steps out of line. The managerial élite is self-recruited by the process of co-option in a way that the capitalist class never was and it controls the route to the top by methods which, in comparison, make nineteenth century capitalism look like a society where 'careers were open to talents'.

And what is the Labour Party's answer? Why, a code of conduct for the managers! The Government in discussion with the Trade Unions and employers is to draw up a code of "desirable social practices" to which industry "will be expected to conform. If need be" [how daring can we get?] "this should be given the force of law". At the same time we are told in *Public Enterprise* that the salaries of the managers of nationalised industries must not be "markedly less than those for similar jobs in private business". Apparently, it's not that the managers have superior rewards and privileges that the Labour Party objects to: only the way they secure them. These managers really should be more discreet!

* * *

I said earlier that our New Socialists had been reading Burnham. I should have added that they have not succeeded in understanding him. The sheer puerility of Labour's answer to The Problem of Social Power would be incredible if one was not prepared for it by the whole history of the party, both in office and out. A new ruling class is emerging and the party proposes to tame it by formulating (in discussion with the Trade Union bosses and the employers) a code of conduct! If the Labour Party had existed in 1800 no doubt it would have proposed a code of conduct to curb the exploitative powers of the capitalists!

The sad truth of the matter is that the Labour Party cannot be expected to formulate any measures to prevent the emergence of a managerial order. Of the two major political parties in this country, its attitude towards the managers is more ambivalent and on the whole more favourable than that of the Conservative Party which, broadly speaking, still represents *capitalist* interests. In future historical perspective, the Labour Party will appear as the harbinger of the managerial order, while the Conservative Party, as ever, will in time adjust itself to the new social forces. I do not wish to deny that there are elements in the Labour Party opposed to managerialism. A party so broadly based in the working class could not fail to voice in some way opposition to the social revolution of our time. But this voice is muted and, unless a near miracle happens, will be lost in the thunder of approval of the new social order. There are too many men of power in the Labour Party and the Trade Union hierarchy with an actual or potential interest in managerialism to make any other outcome at all probable.

If those in the Labour Party hostile to the managers are to have any effect, they must start at once learning their political ABC. I do not say that they will have to come to school at the anarchists, although that would certainly be desirable. But the basic minimum they must learn is that 'the State' and 'the community' are not equivalent terms and that ownership and control by the State cannot automatically be translated into ownership and control by the community. Moreover, all of Labour's proposals to control the managers are based on the naive assumption that the State and industry are in some way separate entities. The State is to control industry and, by implication, the managers by planning techniques and codes of conduct. But our society at its top levels – as distinct from the middle levels of power – is not a pluralist society, and is rapidly becoming less so every year. The political élite and the industrial managerial élite are merging. The industrial bosses – the Bevins and the Lord Millses – become political bosses and to a lesser extent – significant in itself of the social forces at work – the political bosses become industrial bosses. When the merger is complete, State and industry will be simply different aspects of the same Establishment. The new power élite will then confront the powerless masses: the social revolution will be complete.

Industry and Society is indeed an important document: it points the way to the Managerial Society.

Socialism by Pressure Group

There are two main types of pressure group. One is the group organised to represent and further the interests, usually 'material', of a relatively stable section of a community. Employers' and employees' associations, such as the FBI and the TUC, are the most obvious examples of this type. The other is the group organised to represent and further the interests, usually 'ideal', of a set of like-minded individuals. The essential basis of this second or 'promotional' type is the common acceptance by the group's members of a proposal or set of proposals which they wish to see implemented by the authoritative decision-makers of the society in which they operate. The Anti-Corn Law League, the Anti-Vivisection Society and the CND are all examples of this type. From their very nature, groups of this kind tend to be less stable, more ephemeral than sectional interest groups. The Fabian Society, however, appears to be an exception to this rule. Founded in 1884, it rapidly became, and remains today, the most influential pressure group in the British socialist movement. Its impact on the wider society, if unmeasurable, has been great. Recently, it has been paid the sincerest compliment of all by its Conservative political opponents: imitation. The successful and much-publicised Bow Group of Tories was deliberately modelled on the Fabian Society and designed to combat its influence.

In her latest book,[1] Margaret Cole gives us what amounts to an official history of this socialist pressure group. Soberer, more informative and a good deal more accurate than the journalistic effort of Miss Fremantle which appeared last year,[2] it supplements, if it does not replace, the previous 'official' account by Edward Pease written in 1916.

The general character of Fabianism is too well known to need depicting here. 'Fabian' has long been a term of abuse in the

---

1. *The Story of Fabian Socialism* by Margaret Cole.
2. *This Little Band of Prophets* by Anne Fremantle.

vocabulary of radical socialists and libertarians, ever since its original anarchist members, headed by Kropotkin's collaborator, Charlotte Wilson, were manoeuvred out of the Society in 1887. Mrs Cole, in an epilogue, attempts some assessment of the Society's record but fails to meet, let alone to answer, the most serious charges levelled against it. Committed to being 'practical' and to the pursuit of the municipal and Parliamentary road to socialism, the early Fabians distinguished themselves from their socialist contemporaries by their resolute opposition to 'political luddism' – State-busting – in all its forms. Their successors, despite their avowed *penchant* for political *free-thinking*, have never questioned this commitment. Confronted as we now are by a State in which even the Tories 'plan' the economy – in a manner deliberately designed to win elections – and further away than ever, apparently, from the realisation of a society which anyone with the instincts of a William Morris would recognise as socialist, the Fabians still urge us along the same path. More facts, more tracts, and, so we are assured, all will be well. Frank Horrabin's Fabian tortoise with its uplifted paw – looking like an outraged old-age pensioner begging for a shilling rise to meet the latest increase in the tobacco tax – moves slowly, but move it does. Where it has come from, the historically minded Fabians are quite clear: where it is going to, the unphilosophically minded Fabians have never bothered to enquire.

Seventy-seven years further on from its starting point, perhaps the most interesting question to ask about this organisation is: How has it managed to survive and still be kicking? Part of the answer undoubtedly lies in its relative lack of dogma. The early Fabians saw themselves as the latter-day Benthamites of British socialism. Beyond a few basic principles enshrined in the Society's original Basis, which even some Liberals and Tories found themselves capable of accepting, they had no set programme to foster. Proposals for reform they produced in plenty, many of which have found their way on to the statute books of the State and of local and other authorities. But the Society *as such* promoted none of them. Almost from the start, each proposal was presented with the disclaimer that it represented the views, not of the Society but only of the individual who prepared it. As a consequence, divisions within the membership over specific policy matters, although not avoided altogether, have been kept to a minimum. This organisationally sensible procedure was taken a step further in 1939 when – a new and even broader 'basis' having been adopted – the Society accepted as a fundamental rule the self-denying ordinance which forbade it to put forward any resolution of a political character, expressing an opinion or calling for action, in the name of the Society. This rule immediately placed the Society out of the reach of interested minorities chasing paper majorities which has been the bane of most socialist and labour organisations. No Fabian delegate to any other organisation has a mandate from the Society and his vote commits no one but himself. Freedom from internal political manoeuvring and policy rivalries has left the Fabians with the energy to pursue their major task – research and education. At the same time, it has enabled their Society to attract financial support from a wide variety of sources.

As an organisation, the Fabian Society has also shown a remarkable ability to hive off those groups and individuals within the membership who looked like making trouble. The hiving off of the anarchists in 1887 by the passing of a resolution committing the Society to participate directly in political action – a resolution which the majority had no intention at that time of implementing – was only the first of a series of such events. Before the First World War, the old guard Fabians met a number of challenges to their authority by giving the rebels their head and an organisation of their own. Some of these organisations quickly perished; others, like the Fabian Research Department, subsequently captured by the CP and renamed the Labour Research Department, survived. The peak of the Society's influence was undoubtedly reached before 1914. After 1918 the Fabian's monopoly of socialist cerebration was broken by the establishment of other bodies, including the Labour Party's own research department. In the '20s and '30s, under the bumbling secretaryship of F.W. Galton, the Society went into a decline. By 1939 it was on the point of expiry. But it survived because a few years earlier G.D.H. Cole and his friends had formed the New

Fabian Research Bureau. An amalgamation of the Bureau and the Society, under Cole's leadership, gave it a new lease of life. Membership figures, if not influence, reached a peak in the post-war years. The years of apathy and the lost sense of socialist direction have since eaten into the membership. One no longer looks to the Society in the expectation of finding 'new' socialist thinking, but the volume of work produced remains high and the odd tract here and there warrants a *Times* or a *Guardian* leader.

Part of the success of the Society must also be attributed to the quality of its leadership. The verbal brilliance of Shaw which attracted hundreds and thousands needs only to be mentioned. More important in the long run were the prodigious efforts of that bureaucrat *par excellence*, Sidney Webb, and, more recently, of G.D.H. Cole. That Cole, the guild socialist rebel who plagued the life out of the Webbs in the period 1914-24, should have succeeded to Sidney Webb's mantle seems a bit ironic.

"Mr G.D.H. Cole is a bit of a puzzle, With a Bolshevik soul in a Fabian muzzle." So sang Maurice Reckitt in 1920. Margaret Cole comments that the epigram would have been more correct if 'anarchist' were substituted for 'Bolshevik'. The anarchist element in Cole's thinking was very real and remained with him to the last. So much is evident from the final paragraph in the last volume of his *History of Socialist Thought* where he repudiated both Social Democracy and Communism. The puzzle about Cole remains but there is no doubt that he shared with the Webbs a selfless devotion to the cause of socialism. Neither the Webbs nor Cole, nor many other Fabian stalwarts, were 'on the make'. We may violently disagree with many Fabian policies and principles but it is difficult to point a finger at the men. If only their energies and capacities had been wholeheartedly devoted to the libertarian cause, we might not now have to make such a qualified approval of this most famous of all socialist pressure groups.

Socialism by Pressure Group

Geoffrey Ostergaard's excellent account of the Fabian Society as a socialist pressure group (*Freedom*, 12th August) fails to mention its other function – a front organisation for the Labour Party. Indeed he only refers once to the Labour Party, and then only in passing, which isn't really good enough, even for *Freedom*. It is worth noting that membership of the Society, according to the little note in its frequent publications, "is open to all who are eligible for individual membership of the Labour Party", which effectively excludes anyone who belongs to most other political groups whether to the right or to the left; neither Liberals nor Communists have a chance of taking it over. The note adds that "other radicals and reformers sympathetic towards the aims of the Society may become Associates" (with no voting power, of course). What it does *not* add is that the Society is actually affiliated to the Party, as one of the five 'Socialist Societies' which send four delegates to the Annual Conference and which join the 'Co-operative and Professional Organisations' in putting Arthur Skeffington, MP for Hayes and Harlington, on the National Executive Committee of the Labour Party. More informally, most of the top people in the Fabian Society are top intellectuals in the Labour Party.

The Society is in fact a sort of intellectual debating hall for Party disputes which might get out of hand if they were conducted in the popular press, Transport House, the Annual Conference or the House of Commons. It is at the same time a safety valve for clever malcontents, a kite-flying device for the Party Establishment and a nice dependent-looking façade for left-wing intellectuals who lean towards Social Bureaucracy but can't quite stomach the Labour Party. In its first capacity we see the defence, nationalisation and culture debates ritualised in monthly instalments, which gratify the protagonists while neutralising their rancour; in its second we see the research pamphlets, which are often prepared by members of the Transport House staff to foreshadow policy changes; and in its third we see special treats for uncommitted but sympathetic intellectuals, such as Kingsley Amis's *Socialism and the*

Intellectuals, Wayland and Elizabeth Young's *The Socialist Imagination* – and we might also have seen Michael Young's *The Chipped White Cups of Dover* a year ago if it hadn't stepped too far out of the Party line, by suggesting the idea of "a new progressive party" (its original title) and been narrowly rejected by the Society's Executive Committee for that reason.

Make no mistake, the Fabian Society couldn't survive as a pressure group any longer than its mirror-image, the Bow Group, if it weren't constantly preserved as a front organisation by the Labour Party. It is quite different from the Young Socialists' organisation, which is openly run by the Party bureaucracy, or the New Left movement, which is genuinely independent; it manages to get the best of both worlds, chiefly because it has a tradition of political respectability (not to say downright timidity) which has percolated down to the Young Fabians, and so survives and remains the exception to the rule stated by Geoffrey Ostergaard: that pressure groups are normally highly unstable. The point is that its members can feel that they are more than mere intellectuals or mere politicians, and so salve their fear of political or intellectual inadequacy respectively; at the same time the Party Establishment can feel that it is using the Society rather than the other way round (which is the simple truth), and so salve its fear of either political or intellectual independence. This is why Fabians like Cole are so ineffective when it comes to the point – they can't last any longer in the Society if they oppose the Party than the Anarchists could 74 years ago. Thus the Horrabin tortoise plods on, winning race after race, only to learn too late that the hare changed the rules half-way through.

AF

Fabian and Parliamentary Socialism

In September 1886 the Fabians, as Mrs Cole has recently reminded us, "finally made up their minds on the question of Anarchism versus Parliamentarianism" (Margaret Cole: *The Story of Fabian Socialism*). With the deliberate intention of sloughing off their anarchist wing, the Fabian leaders called a meeting to consider the following resolution: "That it is advisable that Socialists should reorganise themselves as a political party for the purpose of transferring into the hands of the whole working community full control over the soil and the means of production, as well as over the production and distribution of wealth". To this William Morris, the leading libertarian socialist of the day, moved a rider: "But whereas the first duty of Socialists is to educate the people to understand what their present position is and what their future must be, and to keep the principle of Socialism steadily before them; and whereas no Parliamentary party can exist without compromise and concession, which would hinder that education and obscure those principles, it would be a false step to take part in the Parliamentary contest". After a stormy meeting, the original resolution was carried by 47 votes to 19 and Morris's rider rejected by 40 to 27.

This decision, taken in an obscure London hotel room, marked a turning point in the history of British socialism. The Fabian leaders had no immediate intention of implementing their resolution: they were still wedded to the tactic of 'permeating' the existing parties with their socialistic ideas. But it was nevertheless an important symbolic event. For the Fabians were in the process of establishing themselves as the ideologists of a respectable variety of socialism, a socialism different in kind from the then current 'socialism of the street'. And the first principle of this new socialism, differentiating it sharply from both Marxism and anarchism, was a 'resolute constitutionalism', and acceptance of the existing political structure. With characteristic brilliance, Bernard Shaw in an article in *Today*, September 1887, put the case against anti-statism: "I regard machine breaking as an exploded mistake. A machine will serve Jack as well as his master if Jack can get it out of his master's hands. The State Machine has its defects; but it serves the enemy well enough: and with a little adaptation, it will serve us quite as well as anything we are likely to put in its place".

The subsequent history of British socialism is an extended commentary on the naive but persuasive fallacy contained in this passage and a vindication of Morris's judgement that it would be a 'false step' to embark on the Parliamentary road to socialism.

In his brilliant and polemical study of the history of the Labour Party over sixty years (*Parliamentary Socialism, a Study in the Politics of Labour*), Ralph Miliband provides much of the documentation to support this thesis. The perspective from which he writes is not, it must be said, that of an anarchist: he is a Labour Party Leftist in the Laski tradition. But the material he has compiled so industriously and with a keen eye for the revealing quotation is almost pure grist for the anarchist mill.

Integration with Parliament

His main contention is simple and incontrovertible: "The leaders of the Labour Party have always rejected any kind of political action (such as industrial action for political purposes) which fell, or appeared to fall, outside the framework and conventions of the parliamentary system". At each stage in the party's growth, from the time when it was little more than a pressure group in the House of Commons to the time of its transformation into the official Opposition and its subsequent emergence as the government party, the Labour leadership has consciously and deliberately steered the organisation in the direction of its complete integration with parliamentary politics. If in the process the socialist dream of a new order based on co-operative as opposed to individualistic acquisitive social relations has to be discarded, so much the worse for socialism! Complete integration has not even yet been finally achieved but, under Gaitskell's leadership, we may fairly predict that the end is in sight. When a few more manoeuvres have been executed, when the annual conference has at last been transformed into a chorus echoing the chants of the leadership, and when the wild men of the Left have been finally tamed, then the party of Tweedledum will joyfully confront the party of Tweedledee.

Miliband's study is especially valuable because it places the present tensions and strains of the party in historical perspective. The division between the parliamentary leadership and the socialist activists is no new thing: it has been a permanent feature of the party's life. What *is* new about the present crisis is the fact that the fundamental question about the social purpose of the party can no longer be evaded. For a generation after 1918, the year when Clause Four was written into the party constitution, labourite social reformers and socialists could co-exist, albeit uneasily, in the same party. Whatever misgivings they might have about the policies being pursued by the leaders, the socialists could persuade themselves that the direction if not the pace of the party was correct. By the end of the third Labour Government, this illusion was becoming painfully transparent. The moment of truth had arrived. The Labour leadership made it quite clear – and recent revisionism has only underlined it – that by socialism it understood, not a new social order but a regulated Welfare State capitalism. The nationalisation and welfare measures which the militants had seen as the *beginning* of the social revolution was defined by the leaders as being in themselves the social revolution. All that remained to be done was a consolidation of this 'revolution'.

In tracing the perennial conflict between the leadership and the rank and file, Miliband identifies two different sets of critics on the Left. One set which he labels the Labour Left has assumed a variety of forms at different periods – the ILP, 1900-32, the Socialist League in the 1930s, Bevanism and Victory for Socialism in the 1950s. Its purpose has been twofold: to push for more radical policies and to press for more militant attitudes in response to the challenges from Labour's opponents. Although it has accepted the categories of the parliamentary system, it has done so, unlike the leadership, with certain misgivings: its acceptance has been accompanied by "a continuous search for means of escape from [the] inhibitions and constrictions" of the system. The other set of critics Miliband calls "the extra-parliamentary Left for whom parliamentary politics has always been of secondary importance, if that". The most important single group of this kind has been the Communist Party, but Miliband also includes in this set the Social Democratic Federation in its various forms, the SPGB, the Socialist Labour Party, and the syndicalists and industrial unionists. The listing of these diverse groups indicates that Miliband's 'extra-Parliamentary Left' is a residual rather than an analytical category. It comprises, in effect, all Leftist groups outside the Labour Party. In view of the general tenor of his argument, Miliband's failure to consider more carefully the diversities within this set constitutes a serious weakness in his analysis. It is just not good enough to lump CPers, SPGBers *et al* together with the syndicalists and declare that "beyond their more complex differences the simple message they carried was that the wage-earners achieve neither immediate reforms, nor the emancipation of their class, without a militant assertion of their strength outside Parliament". Alone among the groups of the extra-Parliamentary Left, the syndicalist heirs of the anarchist tradition had a clear and well-formulated position *vis-à-vis* Parliamentary and other forms of politics. If Miliband had stopped to consider the syndicalist doctrines, his analysis would have been much more effective.

No effective challenge to the leadership
Miliband's failure in this respect is all the more disappointing, because despite his own sympathies, he is very aware of the shortcomings of the Labour Left. His appraisal of these groups is, in fact, of greater significance than his more familiar criticisms of the official leadership. The Labour Leftists have always been a force the leaders have had to reckon with. On occasions, notably in 1944, they have succeeded in committing the leadership to policies more radical than the latter wished to pursue. But at no time have they constituted a majority within the party. They have seldom posed an effective challenge to the leadership and they have never come near to capturing the Labour Movement's commanding heights of

power. Their victories have been mainly verbal ones which, with few exceptions, have made little difference to the party's conduct inside or outside Parliament. Miliband's judgement on the so-called 'wild men of the Clyde' in the 1920s will stand for the Labour Left as a whole: "They didn't shape the strategy of the party. They only continued as their predecessors had done ... to make its bark appear, at least to the uninstructed, much more frightening than it had ever a chance of becoming under its real controllers".

That this judgement holds good of the successors of the Maxton-Kirkwood group is shown by Miliband's perceptive comments on Bevanism in the 1950s: "Many of the political ambiguities of parliamentary Bevanism were but a reflection of its ideological ambiguities. Throughout, parliamentary Bevanism was a mediation between the leadership and the rank and file opposition. But the parliamentary Bevanites, while assuming the leadership of that opposition, also served to blur and to blunt both its strength and its extent. Themselves limited by their parliamentary and executive obligations, they fell back on the politics of manoeuvre, and were regularly outmanoeuvred in the process".

If we accept, as I think we must, Miliband's judgements on the Labour Left, we are forced to ask ourselves the question which the author comes near to posing but does not actually pose himself: Is there any real future for the Labour Left? Despite a few optimistic signs in recent years – the emergence of the New Left groups, the persistence of 'radical' views, especially on public ownership, even within some of the more conservative-minded trade unions – the prospect of the Labour Left becoming anything more than a nuisance to the leadership remains dim. And if this is the prospect, the Leftists must ask themselves: What useful purpose is now served by their remaining in the party?

In discussing Bevanism, Miliband rightly points out that the Bevanites were mistaken in thinking that their cause was furthered by the victories they secured in the National Executive and Shadow Cabinet elections. These successes imposed on the victors an acceptance of policies which they had no chance of affecting in any significant way. Bevanite membership of the NEC made it more, not less, difficult for them to give effective direction to the struggle against Right-wing policies. An important political truth is involved here. One of the most effective ways a ruling group can disarm its opponents is to 'co-opt' the rebel leaders into the group, thus compelling the rebels to accept some measure of responsibility for the ruling group's policies. From the Labour leadership's point of view, they would no doubt have preferred to have bought over the Bevanite leaders by promises of jobs, 'concessions', etc., but failing that, 'co-option' by democratic election was the next best thing.

The Leaders need the Left

But if this argument is valid in this particular context, is it not equally valid in a wider context for the Labour Left in relation to the party as a whole? By remaining in a party which they have no real prospect of controlling, the Labour Left serves only to legitimise the policies of the leadership, to make them more acceptable than they would otherwise appear. Without the presence of the Left, the Labour leaders could not delude the unsophisticated rank and file into thinking that the party was an instrument for the achievement of socialism. It is a mistake to believe that the Labour leaders want to get rid of the Left by expelling them *en bloc* from the party: the leadership's interests are best served by a Left that is both within the party and safely under control. In this way, the party can enjoy the benefits without the disadvantages of Leftism.

From the long-term historical perspective, it is naive of Leftists to fulminate against the leaders of the Labour Party for their 'betrayal' of socialism: if there has been any betrayal, it is one for which the Labour Left must accept a full measure of responsibility along with the leadership.

But 'betrayal' is not the right word. To write, as Miliband does of the leaders of the General Strike and by implication of the whole Labour leadership, that "betrayal was the inherent and inescapable consequence of their whole philosophy of politics" is to reveal one's sociological naiveté. The blurb hails the book as "an historical essay in political sociology". It is nothing of the kind: at most it provides merely the materials for such an essay. One has only to compare

Miliband's book with that classic of political sociology, Roberto Michels's *Political Parties* to see the point. The comparison is the more apt since it was Michels who made the observation, fifty years ago, that "the socialists might conquer, but not socialism, which would perish in the moment of its adherents' triumph". Assuredly, the Labour Party's development would not have surprised Michels! But there is no evidence that Miliband has absorbed the lessons of Michels.

What makes Michels's book an essay in political sociology is the fact that he looks for an explanation of political behaviour in terms of social structure. Miliband, in contrast, and despite his broadly Marxist orientation on issues like public ownership, offers a 'liberal' explanation in terms of ideas. Having carefully traced a persistent pattern in which the behaviour of the leaders is sharply opposed to that of their Left critics, he accounts for this pattern, in effect, by saying that the leaders had the wrong ideas – that they were wedded to parliamentarianism and all its conventions and to social reform rather than to socialism. This, of course, is true but not very illuminating. What one wants to know is *why* the leaders behaved as they did and equally *why* they found themselves continually confronted by frustrated Left critics.

Function determines behaviour

A *sociological* answer to this question would begin with Michels's theory of 'the iron law of oligarchy', with its implication that the very creation of a complex mass organisation unleashes 'conservative' forces. And it would explain the perennial failure of the Labour Left by the fact that in such organisations the control of decision-making for a variety of reasons, such as superior access to the means of communication, tends to concentrate in the hands of the leadership. The answer might proceed by distinguishing the different *roles* of the leaders and the militants. It is an axiom of sociology that to a large but indeterminate extent the behaviour of individuals is determined by the roles they perform. The leadership role is clearly different from that of the militant rank and file and the ideas of both may be largely a reflection of their respective roles.

For example, one of the functions of the leadership is to preserve the integrity of the organisation without which they would not be leaders. The leaders are much more concerned with this question than the militants and at least part of their 'conservative' behaviour may be explained by their desire to 'conserve' the organisation. The present Labour leadership believes – and all the evidence suggests 'quite correctly' from the short run point of view – that a programme of further extensive public ownership would react unfavourably on the party's electoral prospects. Revisionism is not merely a matter of ideas: it has its roots in the social structure.

Nor should it be forgotten that the leaders of an alternative government party perform roles not only in the party but also in the state organisation. Their state roles, either actual or potential, are in fact their most important roles. In performing these roles, the leaders inevitably find themselves constrained by forces in the state over which they have only limited control. When you find socialist governments making concessions to big business or socialist Colonial Secretaries pursuing imperialist policies, these are not necessarily due to wrong ideas or defects of character: the pursuit of such policies may be the only course open to them if they are to remain in office. For the radical, a sociological explanation of Labour politics would lead to the conclusion, not that the Labour leaders have 'betrayed' socialism and that all might yet be well if only they could be persuaded or compelled to adopt a genuinely socialist programme, but that socialism cannot be brought about by Parliamentary means. As William Morris saw, "no Parliamentary party can exist without compromise and concession" and the price of trying to achieve socialism through such a party is and must be compromise and concession.

For some readers, Miliband's demonstration of the failure of social democracy in Britain will suggest the moral that the way to socialism lies through a party of the Communist type. The kinds of tactics and strategy that he appears to favour have always been espoused by the Communists and it is true that Communist parties have managed to play the political game without becoming disastrously infected by parliamentarianism. But Communist success – not of course in Britain but elsewhere – has been achieved only by the creation of a dictatorial type of organisation, Communist parties, unlike social democratic parties, can achieve the forms of a socialist society but neither can achieve socialism in the classical sense of a free classless society. It is a possibility that has to be faced that there is *no* road to such a society. But, if there is one, all experience of the last fifty years suggests that it is the third road pioneered by the anarchists and syndicalists. In Britain today there is a greater interest than there has been for two generations in this third road – the road of direct as opposed to political action. If Miliband's book, for all its shortcomings, stimulates this interest, it will have served a purpose even more useful than that intended by its author.

Modernity and its Aftermath – British Syndicalism: End of an Era?

In the aftermath of the decline of British trade unionism since 1985 we need to consider the place of radical syndicalism, as recommended by Geoffrey Ostergaard, in what has been called the post-modern society. To do this we need an overview of how and why syndicalism developed historically and to consider if it has reached an historical dead-end.

If we go back to the early days, G.D.H. Cole in his essay 'Attempts at General Union 1829-1834' said that those actively involved in the Grand National Consolidated Trades Union (GNCTU) of 1833-34 were mainly in those trades not yet absorbed by the industrial revolution. One implication here is that the GNCTU, though large (perhaps half a million strong), was dominated by politically has-been trades, farm labourers and artisans, creatures of the pre-industrial age rather than factory workers. In his book *The Common People* G.D.H. Cole declares: "The trades it [the 'Grand National'] covered included farm-workers, miners, tailors, gas-workers, shearmen, sweeps, bonnet-makers and bakers". Many trade clubs joined almost automatically, but it is doubtful if they paid full contributions on all their membership.

Here was an organisation devoted, according to E.P. Thompson, to the "theme ... of industrial syndicalism", while Karl Marx was still a lad. And Mr Thompson adds: "Hence the workers who had been 'insolently placed without the pale of social government' developed stage by stage a theory of syndicalism, or of 'inverted masonry'." (*Man*, October 1833). At that time 'A Member of the Builder's Union' wrote: "The trade unions will not only strike for less work, and more wages, but will ultimately *abolish wages*, become their own masters and work for each other; labour and capital will no longer be separate but will be indissolubly joined together in the hands of workmen and work-women."

Geoffrey Ostergaard tends to pass over what he calls "the dramatic collapse of the Grand National" in 1834. But did this radical syndicalist notion of a revolutionary transformation of society represent the deranged fantasy of a pre-industrial age? Some Marxists argue that it did!

An alternative argument is that the workers then, who had not been swallowed up whole by the industrial revolution, could make critical comparisons between the factory system and what preceded it. At critical moments Spain, Russia and Mexico seem to have experienced a similar clash between the peasants and artisans, and modernity. In England in the nineteenth century E.P. Thompson, discussing our "radical culture" in *The Making of the English Working Class*, says: "True enough, one direction of the great agitations of the artisans and outworkers, continued over fifty years, was to resist being turned into a proletariat. When they knew that this cause was lost, yet they reached out again in the '30s and '40s, and sought to achieve new and only imagined forms of social control." According to him, at that time the workers constantly complained that 'they wish to turn us into tools' or 'implements' or 'machines'.

One hand-loom weaver witness in 1835 told a parliamentary committee that the workers of England viewed "the Reform Bill as a measure calculated to join the middle and upper classes to government, and leave them [the workers] in the hands of government as a sort of machine to work according to the pleasure of government". Clearly the workers were not marching blindly into the modern world. The poor had been driven off the land by the Enclosure Acts, and daughters herded into the industrial cities lost cooking skills and the ancient recipes of their mothers. Yet these labouring men did not graduate overnight from peasantry into proletariat. They still had that critical capacity to challenge capitalism, the factory system and the oncoming modernity. As E.P. Thompson writes: "They suffered the experience of the Industrial Revolution as articulate free-born Englishmen".

Mr Thompson, who was apprenticed to Marxism, argued that after the "terrible defeats of 1834 and 1835" the vision of the Grand National Consolidated Trades Union was lost, and "the workers returned to the vote, as a more practical key to political power".

Others, anarchists perhaps, would not see this as progress. In her book *Felix Holt – the Radical* (1866) George Eliot had Felix Holt say: "And if any working man expects a vote to do for him what it can never do, he's foolish to that amount ..." and adds "the way to get rid of folly is to get rid of vain expectations".

The growth of the big cities and the development of large-scale industry has tremendous impact on the mentality of the workers. The shift from the artisan's workshop to the big factories may increase class awareness, but it takes away the taste for individual action. The worker in the big factories is good at solidarity in mass actions, but lacks the ability to take individual initiative in small groups. The novelist Ignazio Silone elaborated this point: "The factory worker is a mass-man *par excellence*. It is no accident that in Italy fascism met armed resistance and lost more victims in the regions and cities where large industry doesn't exist and where workers are employed in small enterprises. Compare the respective attitudes of the Spanish workers and the Germans. The difference in character can explain only in part the different way of reacting to the enemy's attack. The growth of big industry has been a powerful help in reinforcing the tendency of Germans – workers included – towards *zusammen-marschieren*. Their inter-party struggles are essentially struggles between different machines. Individual initiative has been reduced to zero." (*School for Dictators*)

What goes for Germans to some extent goes for the law-abiding English, in so far as we were a highly industrialised society. Making some allowance for our differing national character. The fall into industrialised modernity was increasingly marked by rear-guard actions and political reforms beginning with Chartism. In the end trade unionism was merely reactive to the measures of governments and employers – the miners' strike of 1984-85 was initially a struggle to save the status quo in response to government plans to close pits.

In Britain it developed this defensive tradition early on in the nineteenth century, as E.P. Thompson writes: "Hence these years appear at times to display not a revolutionary challenge but a resistance movement, in which both the Romantics and the Radical craftsmen opposed the annunciations of Acquisitive Man". But the Romantic criticism of Utilitarianism remained separate if parallel to that of the craftsman. No one after William Blake was up to the job of interpreting the two traditions to each other.

Hence the working class were left to run the course of history like rats in a treadmill. Of course the voice of syndicalism, or 'inverted masonry', echoed through the nineteenth century as George Eliot records through Felix Holt: "I have the blood of a line of handicraftsmen in my veins, and I want to stand up for the lot of the handicraftsmen as a good lot, in which a man may be better trained to all the best functions of his nature than if he belonged to the grimacing set who have visiting cards, and are proud to be thought richer than their neighbours." Or later when she wrote: "Felix ... contended that universal suffrage would be equally agreeable to the devil; that he would change his politics a little, having a larger traffic, and see himself more fully represented in parliament."

In some countries – Spain and France in particular – the anarchists developed a strategy of anarcho-syndicalism to come to grips with the problems of modernity and capitalism. In Spain, at the start of the century, Gerald Brenan, in *The Spanish Labyrinth*, claimed the adoption of anarcho-syndicalism and the foundation of the CNT rescued the anarchist movement there. But in Britain, just as in the last century the Romantics like "Wordsworth and Coleridge had withdrawn behind their own ramparts of disenchantment", so most of the anarchists held aloof from syndicalism and the workers' movement.

This left the field open to what some have called the Jacobin tendency in politics; the centralisers, the communists, the marxists and state socialists. Without a libertarian or anarchist input, trade unions in Britain remained muscle-bound; a kind of lobotomised labour movement. The syndicalist tradition continued, of course, but as a negative force – a truculent twin of managerialism.

Modernity brought what Wyndham Lewis in *The Art of Being Ruled* called "the great development of associational life", and syndicalism is part of this associational habit of mind.

When I think of the distinction between 'anarchism' and 'syndicalism', I have in mind two types of strike I took part in. In 1964 I was involved in a national strike of engineering apprentices organised by the Apprentice Wages and Conditions Committee. The strike was organised in Manchester and planned for November 1964. There were a number of militant apprentices of different political persuasions on the Committee in August of that year. Before November the committee had split, with a group from the then Socialist Labour League (Trotskyist) breaking away and forming their own committee. This committee then called for a rival strike on a different and later date. The Communists and Trotskyists on the original Manchester committee had fallen out and proceeded to strike-break and scab on each other's respective strikes. The November apprentice strike, which had been planned and plotted at umpteen committee meetings and apprentice conferences, took off in a confused and petty way. Ultimately it ground to a stop when most lads returned to work feeling bitter about being used by the Communist-dominated committee. The Trotskyist-proposed strike held later was even more poorly supported. The anarcho-syndicalist apprentice paper *Industrial Youth*, which was born out of the November strike, continued publication until 1966. The experience was a political horror story in which a strike was planned, plotted and organised according to the principles of traditional syndicalism. That the strike was not a practical success is not surprising. More important in an apprentice strike, it was not a symbolic success and, but for all the recriminations and back-stabbing, it could have been a morale booster for those who took part.

In May 1960 a different kind of strike of engineering apprentices took place. This was reported in *Freedom* by Colin Ward and was in most respects a more anarchistic strike. It broke out in Glasgow in April and spread south, within weeks it had involved thousands of apprentices all over the country. It was a spontaneous strike which snowballed and was organised on-the-hoof as it spread from town to town. There was no time for back-stairs intrigue, the practical demands of picketing and promoting the strike over-ruled the political prattling. The arguments in the streets, at mass meetings and before the factory gates were about real issues. In the end the strike was a symbolic success, though the apprentices' demands were not met until some months later.

At its worst, as displayed in the 1964 apprentice strikes, nothing is more debilitating than the 'associational habit' of modern times.

Henry Ford, mass production, state socialism and the economies of scale, plus the increasing influence of experts, managers and scientific fundamentalists, throughout most of the twentieth century was bound to favour the creation of a more authoritarian syndicalism or trade unionism. Marxist-Leninism, Scientific Management, Fascism and Nazism – the Jacobin tendency came into its own in this century. No wonder Geoffrey Ostergaard called on anarcho-syndicalists to try to keep their 'foot in the door' before it closed forever on industrial freedom.

Yet Mr Ostergaard's problem is the occupational disease of most modern historians – that is a faith in human evolution. Running through most of his writings is the extrapolation of cheerful anticipation, of wishful thinking, a belief in pending progress. But was the miners' strike of 1984-85 any more enlightened a spectacle than the uncontrolled and disorganised disputes that followed the foundation of the Grand National Union in 1833-34? Has Arthur Scargill's mixed-up marxist dialectical-materialism been any more inspiring than the muddled morality of Robert Owen's nineteenth century proclamations of the 'new moral world'? Mr Scargill hasn't got a libertarian-socialist bone in his body and is an authoritarian in both means and ends. Mr Owen may have had more than a touch of megalomania which helped doom the 'Grand National', but 'Owenism' will probably have had longer-term influence than 'Scargillism' ever will.

If anarcho-syndicalism is anarchism's concession to modernity, in the same way Herbert Read's glorification of mass produced art is an anarcho-aesthetic concession to modernism, then it is an attempt to render industrial relations relevant to an anarchist agenda. Or rather make the anarchist agenda relevant to large-scale industry.

But what of anarcho-syndicalism now? Now we are supposed to be in a post-Ford, post-modern world! Now that modernism has reached a dead-end! With manufacturing industry in Britain seeming in terminal decline, and ever-lengthening dole queues, what will become of trade unionism now in a time of 'temps', casuals and freelance workers?

Some contributors to *Freedom* suggest anarcho-syndicalism is a clapped-out vehicle. Others, like syndicalist Derek Pattison, have argued anarcho-syndicalism needs modifying to meet the new era. In a recent pamphlet (*Syndicalism: in Myth and Reality*) Larry Gambone, a Canadian, admits "a revitalisation of *traditional syndicalism* (i.e. separate unions) seems an unlikely future prospect". But he thinks syndicalist ideas will remain influential, and that possibly "a new form of syndicalism may arise" based on professional associations steeped in the culture of the new knowledge-based economy. He proposes that "these associations may also become a force for de-bureaucratisation and workers' control".

In a recent debate of anarchists in the north of England, Derek Pattison asked: "Isn't anarchism part of modernity as well as anarcho-syndicalism?" Yes, anarchism is modern in so far as it applies itself to the modern world through movements like syndicalism, and Sir Herbert Read's criticisms and intellectual ministrations in modern art (Read held that an anarchistic form of society is compatible with a high level of technology). Earlier movements like Robert Owen's 'Grand National' were attempts to harness industry and modernity and render them available to community control and the values of a pre-industrial, pre-modern age of craftsmen and landless labourers.

Yet anarchism transcends modernity! It was certainly pre-modern, and come the day it is capable of evolving a post-modern agenda. That anarchism is a primordial phenomena is a point made by the historian and critic of anarchism A. Ramos Oliveira in his book *Politics, Economics and Men of Modern Spain 1808-1946*: "In a word, anarchism was the moral and political reaction typical of a primitive proletariat, whether rural or urban".

Claiming that anarchism is a social phenomenon which pre-dates anarchist philosophy, Señor Oliveira argues: "Anarchism was the *primordial and elementary manifestation of the discontent of the exploited*".

Anarcho-syndicalism is one attempt to address the modern world after the industrial revolution. I don't think Geoffrey Ostergaard tackled this aspect of social development in modern society. But if the industrial system has changed irrevocably, if the 'modern' has been replaced by the 'post-modern', then the primordial aspect of anarchism in the human condition – the demand of people to control their own lives – will still re-assert itself. The question is what form will this re-emergence take?

Appendix I: What's to be Done

Now that the Anarchist movement has taken a firm hold on what the sturdy old rebel Chatterton is pleased to call the 'disunited kingdom', comrades are asking themselves what they can do to help forward the movement; how they can best work for the establishment of that free condition of society which they so earnestly desire. The answer to the question was given at the conference held at the hall in Lamb's Conduit Street on the 25th of last October. The key note of the new policy was struck on that memorable occasion and we are so satisfied of this and so pleased with it ourselves that we think the date might well be borne in mind for anniversary purposes. If the policy then proposed is acted upon with energy and determination, we feel sure that there will be every reason to celebrate the date by a public meeting this year at which we may record the progress we have made during the twelve months and get up steam for another burst of propaganda in the ensuing year.

Anarchists, in fact, must avail themselves of the trade unions. In other words the trade unionists must be converted to anarchy. This is by no means a very difficult matter. There are now a great many trade unionists who are also anarchists. Let them start on the job at once. They have an admirable manifesto ready for circulation, which is calculated to awaken thought and prepare the ground for them to converse with and thoroughly bring around their fellow workers. Moreover the trade unionist is naturally inclined towards anarchism, towards the principle of working out his own emancipation without having recourse to parliament and the legislators. The trade unionist class is in fact the most self-reliant and energetic portion of the workers. By means of their organisations, we, or rather they, can certainly do very much to lay the foundations of the new society. If it appears to some of us that they are at present as a body rather inclined towards parliamentary methods, let us not forget that this is due to the fact that the Social Democrats have been working amongst them for years and turning their ideas in the direction of state help. Their real inclination, however, is towards independent action. It is an undeniable fact that the basis on which all existing trade unions were founded was self help, defence against the extortions of the capitalist class. In most cases the leaders were strong advocates of direct action and it was only when they became imbued with the spirit of officialism, had made positions for themselves and aspired to parliamentary honours, that they turned away from the old traditions of the movement. This is still to be seen in the action of the present leaders of the older trade unionism and their differences with the leaders of the 'new' unionism. The former having been corrupted by their intercourse with the capitalist class, though they cling to the old ideas of independence refuse to act upon them, thus justifying the criticism of the new school, who profess to be anxious to pass all sorts of acts of parliament for the benefit of the workers. What we anarchists have to do at this juncture is simply to take up the work where the old, corrupted leaders have left off, to continue the movement but at the same time to give it a broader, wider, more complete ideal, to point out the imperfections of the existing unions and how they may be remedied.

Of course there is much in the existing trade unions which is objectionable. They are far too centralistic in their tendency, the ordinary worker has no means so large a share of influence as he should have. They are often not managed on sufficiently broad lines. In many unions difficulties are put in the way of workers gaining admission. They are too much inclined to rest on their oars, that is to say they are not sufficiently aggressive, and the official is far too powerful. But all these and the other defects which might be mentioned, are comparatively insignificant. Unions are free spontaneous associations of working men and women waiting to do anarchistic work. The great fault to be found with them is that the economic education of their members is too far back, that their ideal is too narrow. What is that ideal? Merely to defend themselves against the exactions of the capitalist class, to obtain a minimum wage and in some cases to pay a small 'out of work benefit'. This should be altered. They are already discontented: they must be inspired with the anarchist ideal of being their own employers, their own masters. They must realise that if the worker is to be a free man he must be a joint owner with his fellows of the means of production, and that to obtain the control of these is the end and aim of the labour movement.

To the most men amongst the mass of trade unionists the thought has never occurred that it lies in their power to create a new state of society in which co-operation will be substituted for competition and in which the exploiting middleman between the producer and the consumer will have disappeared. Once this ideal is explained to them in such a fashion as they will readily understand, they will be only too eager to work for it themselves and to enrol themselves under the banner of anarchism. Here and there the idea is even now finding ground, but only as a sort of resource for the unemployed members. For example, the busmen have recently held one or two meetings at which it was proposed that their union should start a few buses so that the unemployed and boycotted members might have employment provided for them. Here again we see the germ of the idea which we anarchists ought to put clearly before the workers. What we have to convince them of, however, is that they should aim not merely at starting business 'on their own hook' for the purpose of establishing a refuge for the unemployed and boycotted members, but that they should seek to eliminate the capitalist altogether; that they should not only feel a spirit of solidarity with their fellow unionists but with all workers, that is to say that each trade should look upon it as their business to find employment for all the workers, inside or outside the union, in their particular trade; that they should consider themselves responsible, as indeed they are, for there being unemployed men in their line of business, and seek to provide employment for them. Once this spirit of universal solidarity and this new ideal begins to be generally accepted, the unemployed question, the black-leg question, the overtime question, the eight-hour day question, and all the subsidiary matters in which workers interest themselves will solve themselves. For when the union and the unionists understand that the unemployed men of their trade are a burden upon them, that they must be either supported by the funds of the society, or in other words out of the pockets of the members, or that work must be found for them, the workers will begin to see that it is against their personal interest if they work long hours and overtime whilst others are not working at all. If there are a large number of men dependent upon the union, a movement will immediately arise in favour of a strike to reduce the hours of labour, not merely to eight, but to such a degree as will find employment for the unemployed men. Once the workers get controlled by this spirit of solidarity, the capitalist will find himself in an impossible position, for he will be unable to make a profit. There being no longer any black-legs, strike must necessarily be successful and the survival of the fittest will result in his being crushed out of existence as capitalist, to be converted, if he is a wise man and accepts the position philosophically, into a fellow-worker enjoying the blessings of a higher civilisation in common with the rest of mankind.

The first thing to be done is to encourage the decentralisation movement. Small unions, federated if the members desire it, are the most effective and give the fewest opportunities to scheming ambitious officials. A very great many of the workers see the dangers of officialism and continual grumbling goes on, but they also see the necessity for organisation. A little discussion, a little thrashing out of the subject with these discontented ones and the anarchist trade unionists will very soon have a host at their back. And this leads us to the question of economic education, one of primary importance. We would suggest that the different unions should be urged to start educational meetings, or that anarchist unionists should start educational meetings themselves, specially addressed to the members of their union. We shall do all we can to help in the matter by the publication of articles, specially dealing with such matters as require elucidation in order to gain over the trade unionists, and by advertising and noticing such meetings. In this connection we would earnestly invite our readers who are trade unionists to send us all the information they can, to report their personal progress in the way of propaganda, to let us know of such difficulties as they encounter, to make arrangements for our speakers to address their members, and in a word to keep us thoroughly well-informed at the same time that they demand from us such aid as we are able to give. There is also a desire amongst unionists to modify the power of their representatives at congresses and conferences and to make them rather delegates carrying out instructions than representatives who say and do as they choose rather than as those who have sent them there desire. This feeling ought specially to be encouraged, even if it is only that the workers may be induced to gather together more frequently and to discuss their own affairs, instead of leaving them in the hands of a few individuals.

This sort of work may seem very prosaic and insignificant to some of our comrades, but it is work that has to be done, of that there can be no doubt. By helping to convert the trade unionists to anarchy you will be laying the foundations of the new society and preparing for the impending struggle. When once the trade unionists get hold of the anarchist ideal and enlarge their unions so as to include all the workers, agricultural, industrial and clerical, and there is no longer any excuse for a man being outside the guild of his calling, the differences between the workers and the exploiters will be forced to a head, the landlords and capitalists will be compelled to stand aside and let the workers have free access to the materials and tools which are necessary to their living happy lives. Then doubtless will come a struggle, but it will be one in which the force and the victory will be on the side of the workers.

February 1892

Appendix II: Anarchism and Syndicalism

The question of the position to be taken in relation to the Labour movement is certainly one of the greatest importance to anarchists.

In spite of lengthy discussions and of varied experiences, a complete accord has not yet been reached – perhaps because the question does not admit of a complete and permanent solution, owing to the different conditions and changing circumstances in which we carry on the struggle.

I believe, however, that our aim may suggest to us a criterion of conduct applicable to the different contingencies.

We desire the moral and material elevation of all men; we wish to achieve a revolution which will give to all liberty and well-being, and we are convinced that this cannot be done from above by force of law and decrees, but must be done by the conscious will and the direct action of those who desire it.

We need, then, more than any the conscious and voluntary co-operation of those who, suffering the most by the present social organisation, have the greatest interest in the Revolution.

It does not suffice for us – though it is certainly useful and necessary – to elaborate an ideal as perfect as possible, and to form groups for propaganda and for revolutionary action. We must convert as far as possible the mass of the workers, because without them we can neither overthrow the existing society nor reconstitute a new one. And since to rise from the submissive state in which the great majority of the proletariats now vegetate, to a conception of anarchism and a desire for its realisation, is required an evolution which generally is not passed through under the sole influence of the propaganda; since the lessons derived from the facts of daily life are more efficacious than all doctrinaire preaching, it is for us to take an active part in the life of the masses, and to use all the means which circumstances permit to gradually awaken the spirit of revolt, and to show by these facts the path which leads to emancipation.

Amongst these means the Labour movement stands first, and we should be wrong to neglect it. In this movement we find numbers of workers who struggle for the amelioration of their conditions. They may be mistaken as to the aim they have in mind and as to the means of attaining it, and in our view they generally are. But at least they no longer resign themselves to oppression nor regard it as just – they hope and they struggle. We can more easily arouse in them that feeling of solidarity towards their exploited fellow-workers and of hatred against exploitation which must lead to a definitive struggle for the abolition of all domination of man over man. We can induce them to claim more and more, and by means more and more energetic; and so we can train ourselves and others to the struggle, profiting by victories in order to exalt the power of union and of direct action, and bring forward greater claims, and profiting also by reverses in order to learn the necessity for more powerful means and for more radical solutions.

Again – and this is not its least advantage – the Labour movement can prepare those groups of technical workers who in the revolution will take upon themselves the organisation of production and exchange for the advantage of all, beyond and against all governmental power.

But with all these advantages the Labour movement has its drawbacks and its dangers, of which we ought to take account when it is a question of the position that we as anarchists should take in it.

Constant experience in all countries shows that Labour movements, which always commence as movements of protest and revolt, and are animated at the beginning by a broad spirit of progress and human fraternity, tend very soon to degenerate; and in proportion as they acquire strength, they become egoistic, conservative, occupied exclusively with interests immediate and restricted, and develop within themselves a bureaucracy which, as in all such cases, has no other object than to strengthen and aggrandise itself.

It is this condition of things that has induced many comrades to withdraw from the trade union movement, and even to combat it as something reactionary and injurious. But the result has been that our influence diminished accordingly, and the field was left free to those who wished to exploit the movement for personal or party interests that had nothing in common with the cause of the workers' emancipation. Very soon there were only organisations with a narrow spirit and fundamentally conservative, of which the English trade unions are a type; or else syndicates, which, under the influence of politicians, most often 'socialist', were only electoral machines for the elevation into power of particular individuals.

Happily, other comrades thought that the Labour movement always held in itself a sound principle, and that rather than abandon it to the politicians, it would be well to undertake the task of bringing them once more to the work of achieving their original aims, and of gaining from them all the advantages they offer to the anarchist cause. And they have succeeded in creating, chiefly in France, a new movement which, under the name of 'revolutionary syndicalism', seeks to organise the workers, independently of all bourgeois and political influence, to win their emancipation by the direct action of the wage-slaves against the masters.

That is a great step in advance; but we must not exaggerate its reach and imagine, as some comrades seem to do, that we shall realise anarchism as a matter of course by the progressive development of syndicalism.

Every institution has a tendency to extend its functions, to perpetuate itself and to become an end in itself. It is not surprising, then, if those who have initiated the movement and take the most prominent part therein, fall into the habit of regarding syndicalism as the equivalent of anarchism, or at least as the supreme means, that in itself replaces all other means, for its realisation. But that makes it the more necessary to avoid the danger and to define well our position.

Syndicalism, in spite of all the declarations of its most ardent supporters, contains in itself, by the very nature of its function, all the elements of degeneration which have corrupted Labour movements in the past. In effect, being a movement which proposes to defend the present interests of the workers, it must necessarily adapt itself to existing conditions and take into consideration interests which come to the fore in society as it exists today.

Now, in so far as the interests of a section of the workers coincide with the interests of the whole class, syndicalism is in itself a good school of solidarity; in so far as the interests of the workers of one country are the same as those of the workers in other countries, syndicalism is a good means of furthering international brotherhood; in so far as the interests of the moment are not in contradiction with the interests of the future, syndicalism is in itself a good preparation for the Revolution. But unfortunately this is not always so.

Harmony of interests, solidarity amongst all men, is the ideal to which we aspire, is the aim for which we struggle; but that is not the actual condition, no more between men of the same class than between those of different classes. The rule today is the antagonism and the interdependence of interests at the same time: the struggle of each against all and of all against each. And there can be no other condition in a society where, in consequence of the capitalist system of production – that is to say, production founded on monopoly of the means of production and organised internationally for the profit of individual employers – there are, as a rule, more hands than work to be done, and more mouths than bread to fill them.

It is impossible to isolate oneself, whether as an individual, as a class or as a nation, since the condition of each one depends more or less directly on the general conditions of the whole of humanity; and it is impossible to live in a true state of peace, because it is necessary to defend oneself, often even to attack, or perish.

The interest of each one is to secure employment, and as a consequence one finds himself in antagonism – i.e. in competition – with the unemployed of one's country and the immigrants from other countries. Each one desires to keep or to secure the best place against workers in the same trade; it is in the interest of each one to sell dear and buy cheap, and consequently as a producer he finds himself in conflict with all consumers, and again as consumer finds himself in conflict with all producers.

Union, agreement, the solidary struggle against the exploiters – these things can only obtain today in so far as the workers, animated by the conception of a superior ideal, learn to sacrifice exclusive and personal interests to the common interest of all, the interests of the moment to the interests of the future; and this ideal of a society of solidarity, of justice, of brotherhood, can only be realised by the destruction, done in defiance of all legality, of existing institutions.

To offer to the workers this ideal; to put the broader interests of the future before those narrower and immediate; to render the adaptation to present conditions impossible; to work always for the propaganda and for action that will lead to and will accomplish the Revolution – these are the objects we as anarchists should strive for both in and out of the unions.

Trade unionism cannot do this, or can do but little of it; it has to reckon with present interests, and these interests are not always, alas, those of the revolution. It must not too far exceed legal bounds, and it must at given moments treat with the masters and the authorities. It must concern itself with the interests of sections of the workers rather than the interests of the public, the interests of the unions rather than the interests of the mass of the workers and the unemployed. If it does not do this, it has no specific reason for existence; it would then only include the anarchists, or at most the socialists, and would so lose its principal utility, which is to educate and habituate to the struggle the masses that lag behind.

Besides, since the unions must remain open to all those who desire to win from the masters better conditions of life, whatever their opinions may be or the general constitution of society, they are naturally led to moderate their aspirations, first so that they should not frighten away those they wish to have with them, and next because, in proportion as numbers increase, those with ideas who have initiated the movement remain buried in a majority that is only occupied with the petty interests of the moment.

Thus one can see developing in all unions that have reached a certain position of influence a tendency to assure, in accord with rather than against the masters, a privileged situation for themselves, and so create difficulties of entrance for new members and for the admission of apprentices in the factories; a tendency to amass large funds that afterwards they are afraid of compromising;

to seek the favour of public powers; to be absorbed, above all, in co-operation and mutual benefit schemes; and to become at last conservative elements in society.

After having stated this, it seems clear to me that the syndicalist movement cannot replace the anarchist movement, and that it can serve as a means of education and of revolutionary preparation only if it is acted on by the anarchistic impulse, action and criticism.

Anarchists, then, ought to abstain from identifying themselves with the syndicalist movement, and to consider as an aim that which is but one of the means of propaganda and of action that they can utilise. They should remain in the syndicates as elements giving an outward impulse, and strive to make them as much as possible instruments of combat in view of the Social Revolution. They should work to develop in the syndicates all that which can augment its educative influence and its combativeness – the propaganda of ideas, the forcible strike, the spirit of proselytism, the distrust and hatred of the authorities and of the politicians, the practice of solidarity towards individuals and groups in conflict with the masters. They should combat all that which tends to render them egotistic, pacific, conservative – professional pride and the narrow spirit of the corporate body, heavy contributions and the accumulation of invested capital, the service of benefits and of assurance, confidence in the good offices of the state, good relationship with masters, the appointment of bureaucratic officials, paid and permanent.

On these conditions the participation of anarchists in the Labour movement will have good results, but only on these conditions.

These tactics will sometimes appear to be, and even may really be, hurtful to the immediate interests of some groups; but that does not matter when it is a question of the anarchist cause – that is to say, of the general and permanent interests of humanity. We certainly wish, while waiting for the Revolution, to wrest from governments and from employers as much liberty and well-being as possible; but we would not compromise the future for some momentary advantages, which besides are often illusory or gained at the expense of other workers.

Let us beware of ourselves. The error of having abandoned the Labour movement has done an immense injury to anarchism, but at least it leaves unaltered the distinctive character.

The error of confounding the anarchist movement with trade unionism would be still more grave. That will happen to us which happened to the Social Democrats as soon as they went into the parliamentary struggle. They gained in numerical force, but by becoming each day less socialistic. We also would become more numerous, but we should cease to be anarchist.

E. Malatesta
November 1907

Publisher's Note and List of Sources

'The Tradition of Workers' Control' was serialised in thirteen issues of the anarchist weekly *Freedom* in 1956, and the type kept standing for later publication in book form. During production, fire broke out at the printing works and, as *Freedom* reported (30th March 1957), "Fortunately the alarm was given early and fire damage was limited to one floor of the building. The basement however was flooded ... Geoffrey Ostergaard's 88-page booklet on *The Tradition of Workers' Control*, the printing of which had been completed all but for sixteen pages, is a soggy mass of paper somewhere in the dump. The type for this work has already been distributed. To reprint it therefore means resetting all the type."

In those days of letterpress printing, the expense of resetting was beyond the resources of Freedom Press, and the project was abandoned.

After Geoffrey Ostergaard's death, when consideration was given to the re-issue of some of his writings, Brian Bamford was of the opinion that 'The Tradition of Workers' Control' was well worth reprinting. He has selected several other articles from the same period, and has provided an introduction and a concluding essay to bring the story up to date, and show its relevance to the current 'New Labour'.

There has been space to append two of the articles from *Freedom* mentioned by Geoffrey Ostergaard. 'What's To Be Done' he saw as an important early instance of anarchists in Britain deciding to work within the emerging labour organisations. It is reprinted here for the first time. The article by Malatesta is, we think, timeless as an account of the relationship between anarchism and syndicalism; although it has occasionally been quoted, the full text has been unavailable for many years.

The texts are taken from the versions published in *Freedom*, with the minimum of alterations to regularise spelling, capitalisation and punctuation, and the silent correction of obvious typographical errors. Dates of first publication are given below.

Geoffrey Ostergaard: the official life, by N[icolas] W[alter], *Freedom*, 21st April 1990.

The Tradition of Workers' Control, *Freedom*, 21st April, 5th May to 21st July 1956.

Fabianism and the Managerial Revolution, *Freedom*, 16th and 23rd January 1954.

Industry and the Managerial Society, *Freedom*, 3rd and 10th August 1957.

Socialism by Pressure Group [review of *The Story of Fabian Socialism* by Margaret Cole], *Freedom*, 12th August 1961.

Socialism by Pressure Group [reader's letter signed 'AF'], *Freedom*, 2nd September 1961.

Fabian and Parliamentary Socialism [review of *Parliamentary Socialism: a study in the politics of Labour*, by Ralph Miliband], *Freedom*, 13th January 1962.

What's To Be Done [unsigned], *Freedom*, February 1892.

Anarchism and Syndicalism, by E. Malatesta, *Freedom*, November 1907.

HOW WE SHALL BRING ABOUT THE REVOLUTION
Syndicalism and the Co-operative Commonwealth

by
Emile Pataud and Emile Pouget

with
Foreword by Tom Mann
Preface by Peter Kropotkin
Translated from the French by Charlotte & Frederic Charles
New Introduction by Geoff Brown

How We Shall Bring About the Revolution, written by two of the most important French revolutionary syndicalists of the years before the First World War, was first published in France in 1909 and translated into English in 1913. It is a spirited account, in the form of a novel, of how the authors saw the processes by which they felt the revolution would come about and how the subsequent, transformed society might organise itself.

It is a revolutionary romance, presenting a dramatic scenario of class conflict: the revolutionary working class takes power by means of a general strike; power is seized from the capitalist state and a stateless syndicalist society is created. Through fictional and utopian – in its very form there is no room for defeat – the tactics used to achieve the revolution in the novel are precisely those that the French syndicalists were using at the time: lessons learnt from actual struggles are incorporated, and several incidents are based on real events.

Above all, it is an inspirational work, designed to raise the consciousness of workers as to their own power. It demonstrates the continuing potential of organised labour to transform society in the working-class interest.

published by Pluto Press (distributed by Freedom Press)

xl, 237 pages   ISBN 1 85305 017 2   £3.95

ERRICO MALATESTA
His Life and Ideas

compiled and edited by
Vernon Richards

Historians are unanimous in considering Errico Malatesta (1853-1932) to be the most outstanding anarchist agitator since Bakunin. As one historian put it, "Malatesta ... bridges nineteenth and twentieth century European thought as few of his peers did". Yet apart from a few pamphlets, all his writings were in the form of articles mainly for Italian anarchist journals, and few have ever been published in English. This volume fills the gap and aims at presenting as complete a picture as possible of Malatesta's ideas on the ends and means of anarchism in his own words.

The second part of the volume – 'Notes for a Biography' – seeks to emphasise the aspects of Malatesta's life which illuminate his political thought, rather than offering a chronological account of his activities.

In part three the editor makes his assessment of the relevance of Malatesta for anarchists today.

The appendices include Malatesta's articles against the First World War, and his long article on Kropotkin, a document of historic importance as well as an example of Malatesta's consummate skill as a writer.

310 pages   ISBN 0 900384 15 8   £5.00

FREEDOM PRESS
84b Whitechapel High Street, London E1 7QX

A DECADE OF ANARCHY
1961-1970
Selections from the monthly journal Anarchy

Anarchy was published by Freedom Press and, during the ten years of its existence, it became known as the leading voice of reflective anarchism in the English-speaking world. No fewer than 118 32-page issues were published under the editorship of Colin Ward, and the present volume contains a representative selection of less than ten per cent of all that material, chosen, arranged and introduced by him.

The thirty items included are classified under seven headings: 'Restatements', in which a number of anarchists seek to link anarchist thought to the contemporary scene; 'Experiences', which are descriptions of the human condition in different parts of the world as witnessed by the writers; 'Work', consisting of four detailed essays ranging from the practical experience of the Gang System in Coventry to the theoretical future of work and including two articles by Geoffrey Ostergaard; 'Education', the ever-topical subject, with contributions from Paul Goodman and Harold Drasdo among others; 'Deviance', yet another burning topic of the day, with contributions from Tony Gibson and Stan Cohen; 'Environments', a topic which has assumed increasing urgency ever since; and 'Retrospects', which gives Colin Ward's contemporary discussion of *Anarchy* in *Freedom* and Rufus Segar's account of doing his famous covers.

Colin Ward's introduction describes the conception and creation of the paper and reflects on its relevance two decades later.

283 pages   ISBN 0 900384 37 9   £5.00

FREEDOM PRESS
84b Whitechapel High Street, London E1 7QX

ANARCHISM AND ANARCHO-SYNDICALISM

by
Rudolf Rocker

Rudolf Rocker (1873-1958) was a German gentile who settled in Britain, became involved with the Jewish anarchists, learned Yiddish and edited Der Arbeter Fraint (The Workers' Friend).

After returning to his native country, he was the moving spirit of the International Congress in Berlin in 1922 which led to the formation of the International Working Men's Association.

In 1933 Rocker left Germany to escape Nazi persecution, and settled in the USA where he worked as a writer.

After the outbreak of the Spanish Civil War and Revolution in 1936, the publisher Fredric Warburg of Secker & Warburg asked him to write a book explaining the ideology behind a mass movement of revolutionary syndicalists, and he produced *Anarcho-Syndicalism* in 1938.

This abridged version was first published in 1948, and has been reprinted several times, most recently with an introduction by Nicolas Walter.

After half a century, Rudolf Rocker's account of anarchism and anarcho-syndicalism is inevitably dated in its emphasis and in some particular points, but it remains valuable as a short and clear view of a significant ideology by one of its best-known and best-informed adherents.

48 pages   ISBN 0 900384 45 X   £1.25

FREEDOM PRESS
84b Whitechapel High Street, London E1 7QX

THE IMPOSSIBILITIES OF SOCIAL DEMOCRACY

by
Vernon Richards

The author was for a number of years a member of the editorial group of the anarchist weekly *Freedom*. The title for this collection of articles was suggested to him by a lecture delivered in 1891 by G. Bernard Shaw to an audience of fellow Fabians with the title 'The Impossibilities of Anarchism'. For Shaw the 'impossibilities' of anarchism were not the ends, with which he thought all socialists would agree, but in the methods, which he found much too idealistic and utopian. Be that as it may, for the purpose of this volume is not to discuss Shaw's views on anarchism but to enumerate and illustrate with contemporary material what are, from an anarchist's point of view, the 'impossibilities' of social democracy.

The 30-odd articles have been grouped under four headings, arguing:

That Labour Party 'Socialism' no longer has any connection with socialism as understood by the Fabians in the 1890s or a Tawney in the '20s, or even Attlee in the '30s.

That the struggle within the Party was no more ideological in Bevan's day than it is today with its vocal protagonists for the so-called Left wing. For the author power, office or even just the limelight are the real issues behind the struggles.

That the trade unions are by reason of their structure and function almost always reactionary, hierarchical, conservative establishment organisations and since the Labour Party was in the first place created by the unions to further their interests and still depends on them for its finances, it is not surprising that who pays the piper should call the tune, which is certainly not socialism.

That the means – elections and vote-catching – have, after so many years playing the party political game, resulted in the means becoming the ends. In the process socialism has been sacrificed to the struggle for office and power.

142 pages   ISBN 0 900384 16 6   £2.00

FREEDOM PRESS
84b Whitechapel High Street, London E1 7QX

A SHORT HISTORY OF ANARCHISM

by
Max Nettlau

translated by Ida Pilat Isca
edited by Heiner M. Becker

Max Nettlau (1865-1944) has been called "the Herodotus of anarchism" — its first and greatest historian. His monumental work is a nine-volume *History of Anarchy*, written in German, of which only three volumes were published in his lifetime because of the economic crisis of the 1920s and Hitler's rise to power in 1933.

A Short History of Anarchism, which Nettlau wrote in French in the 1930s, is a condensation of his massive work, here translated into English for the first time.

The eighteen chapters cover the precursors of anarchism, the history of ideas like individualist anarchism, Proudhonism and revolutionary syndicalism, and the history of the world anarchist movement up to 1930. There are bibliographies of periodicals and of books. The editor has added a guide to Nettlau's work and expanded the index to include brief biographical details of the individuals mentioned.

xxiii, 406 pages   ISBN 0 900384 89 1   £9.95

FREEDOM PRESS
84b Whitechapel High Street, London E1 7QX

All the books advertised here can be ordered from your bookseller or direct from Freedom Press (payment with order) post-free in the UK. When ordering from abroad please add 20% towards postage.
(Girobank account 58 294 6905)